Gillies

# A NEW HOUSE IN AN OLD STYLE

*Both the methods and manner used in English
17th century houses have been followed closely,
skilfully and sympathetically in the construction
and treatment of this house, built almost entirely
of local materials, at Bronxville, N. Y., designed
for Henry N. Morris by Lewis Bowman, architect*

# DISTINCTIVE HOUSE DESIGN AND DECOR OF THE TWENTIES

## With Over 500 Floor Plans and Illustrations

*Edited by*
RICHARDSON WRIGHT

DOVER PUBLICATIONS, INC.
Mineola, New York

Published in Canada by General Publishing Company, Ltd., 895 Don Mills Road, 400-2 Park Centre, Toronto, Ontario M3C 1W3.

Published in the United Kingdom by David & Charles, Brunel House, Forde Close, Newton Abbot, Devon TQ12 4PU.

*Bibliographical Note*

This Dover edition, first published in 2001, is an unabridged republication of the work originally published by The Condé Nast Publications, Inc., New York, in 1925 under the title *House & Garden's Second Book of Houses*. Please note that the two pages "Catalogs for the Home Builder" (p. 114) and "Addresses of Contributing Architects" (p. 191) have been reprinted exactly as they appeared in the original 1925 edition; this information is most likely outdated, but has been retained for research purposes only.

*Library of Congress Cataloging-in-Publication Data*

Distinctive house design and decor of the twenties : with over 500 floor plans and illustrations / edited by Richardson Wright.
    p. cm.
  Originally published: House & garden's second book of houses. New York : Condé Nast Publications, 1925.
    ISBN 0-486-41825-1 (pbk.)
    1. Architecture, Domestic—United States—Designs and plans. 2. Architecture—United States—20th century—Designs and plans. I. Wright, Richardson Little, 1887–1961. II. House & garden. III. Title: House & garden's second book of houses. IV. Title.

NA7208 .D58 2001
728'.37'097309042—dc21
                                        2001047371

Manufactured in the United States of America
Dover Publications, Inc., 31 East 2nd Street, Mineola, N.Y. 11501

# CONTENTS

# MEETING ARCHITECTURE THROUGH THE GARDEN GATE

*This arched entrance occurs in the typically California
house designed for the Ideal Smaller Homes series by
Johnson, Kaufmann & Coate, architects. It leads into
a garden court of which two sides are fronted by the
house and two by a stuccoed wall. Further drawings
of this house are shown on pages 21 to 34*

# A HOUSE OF GRACEFUL DISTINCTION

*Designed after the Georgian Style*
*by Edmund B. Gilchrist*

THE moderately small house has been architecture's stepchild. It has generally been built either with the expanded design of the very small house and clad in the clothes of the large one, or with the reduced designs of the large house and dressed in the manner of its less roomy relative. It has so rarely existed as a house in its own right, with a definite personality and with problems of arrangement and treatment different from every other kind, that when the prospective home owner has thought about the building of a house to cost somewhere between, (say), $20,000 and $30,000, he has hardly known whether to consider a large small house or a small large one. So, partly, this series has been planned to relieve such a perplexity.

The four houses shown on the following pages are distinctly houses of the moderately small type, and in every detail they have been designed as such. But they are much more than that, for they represent the best manners of design and the best methods of construction possible to obtain. Among them may be found the skilful solving of practically every problem which is likely to arise in the planning of the moderately small house. They offer a fine variety of architectural styles without once falling into stereotyped patterns, and they achieve distinction in each style without resorting to trickiness or without striving after the picturesque effects which characterize what has been aptly called "movie" architecture.

Four architects, in different parts of the country, were chosen by HOUSE & GARDEN to prepare these designs especially for this series. All were architects whose work we consider typical of the best that is being done in the way of moderate-size houses in their several localities. They are Richard H. Dana, Jr., of New York City; Edmund B. Gilchrist, of Philadelphia; Howell & Thomas, of Cleveland; and Johnson, Kaufmann & Coate, of Los Angeles. The only conditions attached to our requests for designs were that the house should accommodate a family of at least two adults, two children, and a servant; that it should be set back thirty feet from the front property line and ten feet in from each side line; that it should have a garage attached, and that its cost should not exceed $20,000.

NO MENTION was made of styles. We felt that by giving each architect perfect liberty in this respect he would be able to proceed without any hampering influences and be able to produce something with which he was entirely in sympathy. It was to be expected that each architect would do a house that represented more or less the requirements of his particular region as well as his own taste. These being different in each case, four completely different designs resulted.

The plots, like the houses, are moderately small, being seventy-five by one-hundred-and-fifty feet. Such a space is not only the average suburban lot size but it represents

the probable area which would be developed intensively around a moderately small house regardless of the size of the property. By making one site slope away from the front, one towards the front, and two perfectly level, and then by giving each one a different orientation: one facing north, one south, one west and the other east, we were able to offer for solution all the problems which could possibly come up in planning and grading. With each of the houses on the following pages is shown the bare plot for which it was designed.

The first house shown in this series is a design by Edmund B. Gilchrist along Georgian lines. The architect has not slavishly followed the Georgian style, but has adapted its motifs to a small house of interesting plan and dignified exterior.

The most striking exterior feature is the bow window running through two stories. In it is set the entrance door. Its surface from top to bottom is covered, where it is not glazed, with lead-coated copper sheeting. The lead coating has a smoothly rough texture and quickly takes on a mellow, weathered gray which is extraordinarily beautiful. Like the dormers elsewhere on the house this bow window rises above the line of the eaves and carries an almost flat roof back from its delicate cornice. The ornamental wrought iron scroll set above the cornice on the center of the bow window, as well as on most of the dormers, gives another graceful touch to this finely designed detail. The steep hipped

*The beauty of this house extends well above the eaves which are nicely broken by the decoratively mounted dormers. The steep roof lines are graceful and spirited and the chimneys pleasantly emphatic The terrace, with its wrought iron rail, breaks the change in grade from the first floor level to that of the garden on the slope below*

*The cross part on both of these T-shaped floor plans is largely given over to the service. One end of the living room, large for a house of this size, is used as a dining room. The entrance from the hall into the living room is effectively made down a short flight. At one side of the hall is a study which may be otherwise used as a place for children's outdoor toys*

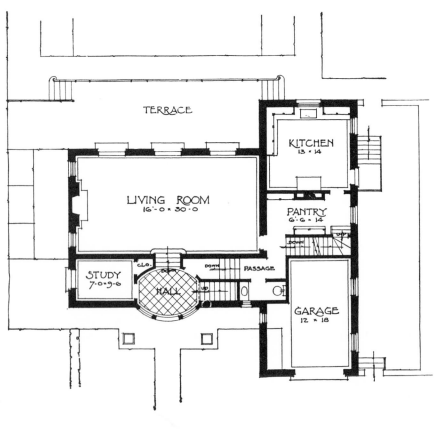

*Mr. Gilchrist's house has a Georgian flavor, faint but fresh. It shows the influence more of an interesting personality than of any particular architectural style*

*The lot slopes away from the front and makes necessary the grading up of the house level to that of the street. From the garden terrace it drops to meet the ground again*

roofs, and the chimneys with their splendid lines, further emphasize the marked individuality of the house.

In the accompanying drawings the house is shown built of brick, but it is a characteristic quality of its design that it would be susceptible to almost any material— weatherboard, stucco, or stone. Many houses—and perfectly justly—rest for their success almost entirely upon the rightness of their materials; they could not easily be imagined clothed in any other thing than that in which they were originally designed. This house depends particularly upon its lines and its graceful masses. With what they are covered is only a matter of intelligent adaptation.

The house is T-shaped in plan, and the cross part of the T is principally given over to the service. From the south east corner of the garage a wall extends to the street, shielding the service entrance from the entrance lawn. Behind this wall are planted a row of Lindens whose symmetrically crowned heads would eventually grow into a solid mass of foliage to show effectively over the top of the high brick wall.

The entrance hall, with its interesting shape, leads into the living room down a short flight of steps; it further leads into a study which might otherwise serve as a room to hold such outdoor toys as velocipedes, bicycles, roller skates and wagons which might else clutter up the entrance; from the right it leads upstairs and off into the service passage. Although the whole house has been kept within fairly small dimensions the living room has been made very sizable. At one end is the fireplace and at the other the space is used at mealtimes as a dining room. To facilitate this purpose a doorway in one corner enters here from the pantry.

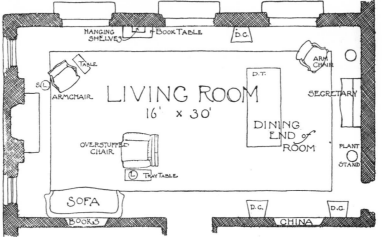

*The fireplace end of the room in the sketch above shows an attractive and livable grouping of furniture. The built-in bookcase is balanced at the other end of the room by a china closet*

*The plan shows the dining end of the room which is furnished with living room pieces. An effective group consisting of a mahogany secretary and two plant stands occupies the end wall*

BECAUSE the house designed by Mr. Gilchrist has something of a Georgian flavor, most of the furniture in the living room is mahogany of 18th Century English inspiration. Mixed with this is a small French occasional table in walnut, a painted book table and a pair of slender painted plant stands. The introduction of these painted pieces brings a nice note of color and is quite in keeping with this type of decoration.

The problem in furnishing this room was to retain an aspect of graceful formality, characteristic of interiors of the Georgian era, in spite of the fact that one end had to serve as a dining room. To keep the appearance of a living room except at actual meal times no typical dining room furniture was used. The mahogany drop leaf table when not in use for meals becomes a commodious living room table, set with a lamp, books, magazines, etc. The secretary at the end of the room is equally at home in a living room or dining room and the graceful Hepplewhite chairs are attractive additions to any interior. Only the open shelves suggest the dining room but even this feature is not out of place and if filled with choice bits of china and an occasional silver piece adds immensely to the decorative and color-ful effect of this part of the room.

The unusual and lovely color scheme chosen for this interior was inspired by the curtain fabric—a semi-glazed chintz with a salmon pink ground and a graceful old-fashioned flower design in henna, mauve, beige and a little hydrangea blue. The paneled walls are painted the same hydrangea blue of the flowers in the chintz with a darker tone rubbed into the grooves of the moldings to take away from the flat look of plain painted surfaces. The color contrast of the salmon ground of the curtains against the pale, hydrangea blue of the walls is one of the most attractive things

*In the long wall space at the dining end of the room is a graceful mahogany secretary. The shelves may be used for books or china and the arm chair can be drawn up to the table at meal times*

*Slender plant stands, painted bluish-green to match the small book table at the right of the fireplace, are used on either side of the secretary at the dining room end*

*The small occasional tray table above is walnut and the lamp is plum colored pottery with a shade of pleated yellow book linen. This is placed between the sofa and chair*

*The fabric used for the hangings in this room is a semi-glazed chintz with a salmon pink ground and an old fashioned flower design in henna, mauve, beige and hydrangea. This material also covers the sofa*

about the living and dining room.

The graceful sofa in front of the book-case is covered in this same material and the comfortable overstuffed chair in front of it has a covering of ribbed cotton material, deep mauve in color. The fabric on the arm chair by the fireplace is artificial silk with a small diamond-shaped pattern in mauve and deep blue. The small table on the right side of the room beneath narrow hanging bookshelves is painted deep bluish green, a lovely color against the hydrangea walls. The rug made of 27″ wide Wilton carpeting is egg plant color and the lamps are plum colored pottery jars with pleated shades of yellow book linen.

The architectural background of the room has the same dignity that characterizes the exterior of the house. Long casement windows are deep set; below them the radiators have been boxed in making window seats. The fronts of these boxes are covered with a wire grille.

The wall treatment simulates

paneling. Panels are marked out with molding set either on the plaster wall or over canvas covered walls. This molding must be delicate enough to be in scale with the size of the room. An abundance of stock moldings offer a wide choice.

Another feature worth noting is the fact that this room lies below the level of the entrance hall and is reached by a short flight of steps. Differences in levels always add to the interest of a house.

The sitting accommodation in the living room end is adequate for five people without drawing on the secretary chair or dining chairs of the other end.

The lighting is also adequate without having recourse to a central fixture. A floor lamp and a table lamp afford light by the sofa and the chairs. Sconces above the mantel give more light when required. A room such as this, however, should be plentifully supplied with floor plugs and movable lamps. When the dining end of the room is used, candles on the tables provide sufficient light.

*This graceful sofa covered in glazed chintz is placed at the left of the fireplace in the living room designed by Mr. Gilchrist*

*The curtains are of semi-glazed chintz with a salmon ground and a flower design in beige, henna, mauve and the hydrangea blue which is also the coloring of the walls*

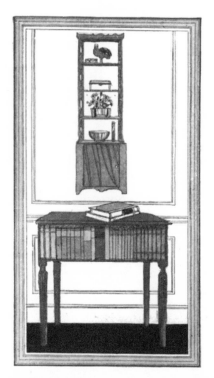

*The side lights are two-bracket electric sconces with crystal drops and a mirror back plate edged with a narrow strip of blue glass. A pair is at each end of the room*

*As will be recalled from the view of the living room end shown on page 10, bookshelves are placed midway down one of the walls. To balance these on the dining room side are the china shelves and linen and silver cupboards*

IN furnishing the combination living and dining room in this house an effort was made to give this interior an appearance of a living room at all but actual meal times. For this reason the furniture selected was mainly of the living room type. The drop leaf mahogany table, which serves as a dining table, is also an excellent size for a living room of this kind, and between meals it holds a lamp, flowers, books, etc. The lovely Hepplewhite chairs are at home in either room and we were fortunate in finding an arm chair that could be used at both the secretary and dining table.

*The reproduction of an old English design is suggested for the china in this dining room. It is white with narrow fluted edge and a fine gold line*

The secretary bookcase at the far end of the room is a type much used in England in dining rooms as well as living rooms. English people live in their dining rooms far more than we do, one end frequently being furnished as a morning room with one or two comfortable chairs and a secretary of this kind. Here the shelves may be used for books or china and the drawers below provide space for the linen not in everyday use.

While the table is being set for meals a screen may be drawn in front of it. However, this is not essential. The reason for thus combining the two rooms is to give one large area.

*The walls of this living-dining room are painted hydrangea blue, a soft background for the furniture at this end—secretary, tall plant stands and the table and chairs. Above is the dining room end in its between-meal state. At mealtimes the table is opened up and the chairs placed. A china closet balances the bookshelves of the living room end*

After all, the dining room "works" but a few hours each day, whereas the living room is constantly in use, and should therefore be given larger space than is generally allotted it in the small house.

A graceful note at this end of the room is the use of slender wooden plant stands on either side of the secretary. These, painted bluish green to match the book table at the other end, are a delightful color contrast to the hydrangea blue walls and mellow tones of the mahogany furniture. Over-door paintings have been suggested in the drawing, but the space can be left to plain paneling. The price of such paintings depending upon the style and the artist has not been included in the price list of furnishings.

Perhaps the most interesting feature of this part of the room is the built-in china closet. This balances the book shelves on the other side of the doorway and in addition to being a decorative note provides the necessary space for china, etc. In place of a large expanse of shelves which, when filled with china present a rather overpowering appearance, the space was divided up into a small open closet with cupboards

on either side and drawers below. Fine bits of china and a few silver pieces may be displayed in the center portion while the other parts can be used for the everyday china, silver and linen. This arrangement insures sufficient space for linen and china that would otherwise have to be kept in the pantry, and it is far more agreeable to look at than an expanse of open shelves.

The china chosen for this room is modern Spode, a reproduction of an old English design. Pure white in color with a fine gold line and a narrow fluted edge, it has the same quality of elegance that distinguishes the rest of the furnishings.

In color this room is both unusual and restful. Against hydrangea blue walls hang curtains of semi-glazed chintz with a salmon ground and a quaint, graceful flower design in beige, henna, mauve, and hydrangea blue. At the living end the sofa is done in this material, one chair in deep mauve rep and another in a sunfast fabric with a small diamond pattern in mauve and blue. This material also covers the arm chair by the secretary, and the Hepplewhite chair seats are done in a heavy cotton ma-

terial in tête de nègre and blue. The lamps are plum colored pottery jars with shades of pleated yellow book linen and the rug is Wilton carpet in a deep egg plant shade. The graceful lighting fixtures have mirror backs outlined by a narrow strip of blue glass, and crystal drops. Such accessories as colored flower prints with narrow blue green frames, an old English silver peony bowl or a Georgian urn shaped silver vase, both charmingly reproduced today, would be effective additions to a room of this kind which is always helped by a glint of silver.

While it might be desirable to furnish such a room in veritable antiques, where one's purse and inclination afforded them, it is possible to have all these pieces in good reproduction. The American furniture manufacturers and the decorators are keenly alive to the demands for good furniture. They are reproducing the best and simple pieces of the past. In such a house as this, in fact, in any American home today, there is no excuse for bad taste in furnishing. Choose furniture of the kind suggested for this room, and your house will be in good taste.

Peach colored walls, furniture painted soft green and chintz hangings in blue, yellow, peach and pink make a colorful and restful bedroom. The rug is made of Wilton carpet in a deep sand tone

This bedroom is so planned that all the necessary pieces of furniture fit in comfortably. By the side of the overstuffed chair is a small tray table, not indicated in the large sketch of the room above

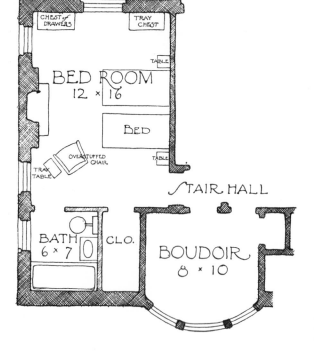

This excellent reproduction of a Queen Anne mirror, suggested for the space over the bureau, has a gilt frame and an engraved design of grapes at the top

The under-curtains in this bedroom are of cream colored net with a narrow stripe and small figure in the design

*If only one bed is used, a Sheraton chair painted green with gold stripings might take the place of the night table. The bed is green with blue lines and the spread blue taffeta bound in peach*

*This small walnut three tier tray table is placed beside the overstuffed chair. The lamp is a cream colored Italian pottery urn with a shade of pleated flowered paper banded in pink*

*On the walnut chest of drawers in the corner between the windows is a pair of lamps made of Dresden pottery shepherdesses in gay colors. The shades are rose chiffon edged with fringe to match*

*The material of the curtains—a semi glazed chintz—supplied the color scheme of the room. It has a soft blue ground and a design of flowers in yellow, peach, pink and green*

THE color scheme of the main bedroom was taken from the fabric of the hangings. This is a semi-glazed chintz with a soft blue ground and a rather formal flower design in peach, yellow, rose and pale green. It was the peach tone of one of the flowers that determined the color of the walls. These and the woodwork are painted a warm yellowish pink, a lovely restful tone and a charming contrast to the blue background of the chintz. The under curtains on the casement windows are cream colored net with a small figure in the design. If preferred, peach colored sunfast organdie might be used.

In order to introduce another color note some painted furniture was used. The twin beds, with their low slender posts and graceful curved headboards, are a soft green, decorated with blue lines—the blue of the background of the chintz. The bedspreads are sunfast taffeta, the same blue, scalloped and bound in peach. Green also are the night tables and combination chest of trays and drawers, shown at the right of the bed. This chest is intended for the man of the family. The lower portion contains two commodious drawers and the upper half is fitted with sliding trays.

On the other side of the window is a chest of drawers in walnut. This is copied after an Italian 18th Century piece and, because of the beauty and simplicity of its design, might be used with equal effect in a living room. Above this hangs a very good reproduction of a Queen Anne mirror with a narrow gilt frame and an engraved design of grapes at the top. The other walnut piece in the room is a small three tier tray table placed beside the overstuffed chair by the fireplace. This table does not appear in the sketch of the room but is shown above. On this page also is illustrated an alternative for a night table in case only one bed is used. This is a graceful chair on Sheraton lines, painted soft green with gold stripings. The small overstuffed chair by the fireplace is covered in the same material as the curtains.

The rug in this room is made of sand colored Wilton carpet.

The extra bedroom in this house has been furnished as a boy's room. A nice contrast to the light coffee colored walls are the red lacquer tones of the picture frames, chair and lamp

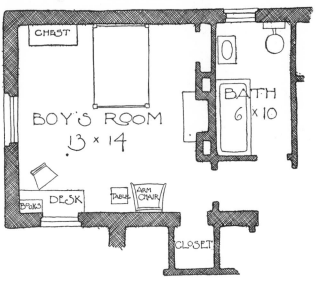

The positions of the various pieces of furniture are indicated in the plan above. If another straight chair is desired it might stand in the space at the right of the bed

A practical feature of the room is the built-in desk and shelves. These provide a cabinet at the bottom for a radio outfit. The graceful small wicker chair is enameled lacquer red

THE tiny boudoir has been made gay with a lattice paper of slender mauve colored leaves on a white ground. The woodwork is painted white and the floor deep violet.

The dominant feature of the room is unquestionably the wide bay window with its graceful, looped back taffeta curtains in a lovely shade of greenish blue. Knife pleated ruffles and a narrow violet piping make these curtains decorative. The under curtains are écru colored net.

Directly in the center of the bay is the dressing table hung in blue and violet taffeta in a graceful petal design. The outer layer of petals is blue and the underneath scallops, which appear for about half an inch, are violet, making a nice line of contrasting color. The edges of both are picoted.

In front of this is a graceful little bench done in striped blue and violet moiré and the covering of the comfortable chaise longue is violet taffeta. A small book table is painted greenish blue and the chenille rug, in the same soft coloring, is usually effective against the violet floor.

Such accessories as crystal lighting fixtures with violet glass pendants, and colored fashion prints framed in black glass provide charming spots of color.

The entrance hall shows what can be done with a small space. At the left as one enters the front door is a door leading to a small study and at the right is the stairway. The only places for furniture are directly in front of the windows on either side of the front door and in the spaces flanking the doorway leading to the living room. Here two slender wrought iron plant stands painted black and gold have been used, and in front of each window is a small, lyre back chair, painted old white. The floor is covered with linoleum in a black and white block design.

A BEDROOM here has been furnished as a boy's room. Furniture copied from early American models in an interesting combination of maple and teakwood, which gives the effect of rather light walnut, has the sturdy appearance essential to a room of this kind.

The walls and woodwork are painted a light coffee color. In striking contrast to this is the note of lacquer red which appears in the hangings, picture frames and lamp. The little wicker chair by the built-in desk is also enameled this gay color, its cushion covered in a two-tone cream striped sunfast material, piped in red. The same fabric makes a simple bedspread.

The window in one corner with its simple curtains of striped cream and

red sunfast taffeta and maple valance board makes a nice background for the built-in desk and gaily painted little wicker chair. The built-in bookcase has a compartment for a radio outfit.

An effective glazed chintz is used for the covering of the one overstuffed chair. It has a blue ground and a quaint design of birds in bright contrasting colors. The lamp on the small table beside the chair is red pottery. The rug is wool Wilton in a deep sand tone and the sconces are dull brass.

*The hall, which occupies the same space as the boudoir above, is made effective by hydrangea blue walls and linoleum is a smart black and white block design*

*A color scheme of mauve and blue has been carried out in this small boudoir. The paper has a lattice design of mauve leaves, and the curtains are blue taffeta*

*Large panel casement windows provide plenty of daylight in the kitchen of this house, thereby making its loveliness more apparent. Rose, gray and white comprise the color scheme*

*The arrangement of the various elements in both kitchen and pantry has been so cleverly devised that confusion cannot exist. All implements, stores and materials are placed where they will be readily accessible*

THE size of this kitchen is thirteen feet by fourteen feet, the pantry six feet by fourteen feet. There is no service room, so the kitchen takes care of all the necessary equipment.

The color scheme: Rose, gray and white, a combination that makes for cheerfulness.

The outstanding things here are the decoratively designed cupboards. In this plan they are of enameled wood. Yet, if you prefer, you can buy any of the excellent kitchen cabinets or units in steel or wood.

There is a solid battleship gray linoleum rubber tile on this floor, which makes it pleasing and unobtrusive.

The working surfaces below the cabinets protrude about 6 inches, giving enough space for working, and there are boards which pull out for greater utility.

This plan has five electric outlets, two electric light switches at the right of all entrances and a large 85-100 ampere central service indirect light.

The ceiling is of French gray and the walls are painted gray. The curtains are rose and white. The woodwork can be white or gray, and the chairs painted too.

Here the refrigerator is electric and highly convenient. But you can have the iced type if you so desire, of course.

The folding table by the wall can be used as a working surface or as a dining table. The outlets near the table make electric toast and waffles on Sunday night an easy performance, which relieves the dining room of extra service.

Again the pantry follows the color scheme of the kitchen. It is built to chime in with the habitudes of the rooms which open off it, the dining room *and* the kitchen. There is ample cupboard space, a sink and serving table, with electric outlets to furnish electricity.

The kitchen sink is of the most modern style. There is a swinging faucet (which can be put in every sink) and slanting drains of porcelain over iron.

There is ample room for a dishwasher attached to the plumbing, so that dishwashing becomes a comfortable thing rather than a baneful bore.

The range is again the most modern of white enameled gas ranges with heat and oven control, self-lighting and beautiful to look upon. It can be had in black or white, of course.

This kitchen is like the rest of the house, of graceful distinction. It would be lovely in green and white instead of old rose, gray and white, with curtains of green and white, leaving the floor the battleship gray.

Of course, when any home is built, the new kitchen ventilating fans in window or flue will take off odors and insure comfort in all weather.

*The site of this house falls fairly sharply from the highway to the rear of the plot,
thus giving opportunity for a succession of descending levels, each one a garden,
and each one separated from the other by a retaining wall of rubble masonry*

*The lowest of the three levels is a simple turf terrace with a low wall towards either end broken with semi-circular steps and a higher wall at the side similarly handled with a pool. This is the last and lowest of the gardens and its shade and walls and water are all that is necessary for making it a pleasant and comfortable sitting place*

SINCE these grounds sloped away from the road, the house level was graded up into a flat lawn. From this house level to rear of the property there is a drop in grade of ten feet. The distance from the flag-paved terrace, on which open the French windows of the living room, to the back line is about seventy-five feet. This area has been divided into three garden terraces each one approximately twenty-five feet wide, separated by retaining walls three feet high.

The treatment of the grounds has been such that they offer two things particularly —seclusion and a rather mild formality. The tall surrounding hedge of clipped Arborvitae (which might be also either Privet or Cedar or English Beech), together with the row of Flowering Dogwoods along the south side of the property, provide the seclusion. Without this enclosure the grounds would need to be planted quite heavily with shrubbery and small trees to prevent the simplicity of their planting from appearing scanty or plain. As it is, the lowest garden has been made unusually effective with scarcely any attempt at planting. It depends for its loveliness upon broad surfaces of turf broken only by two tall Elms, two low retaining walls cut by curved steps, a circular pool set in the wall that separates it from the garden above, and the background of hedge.

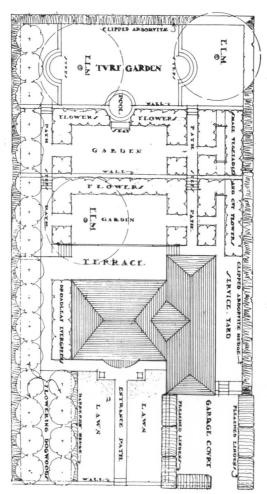

The two gardens on the intervening levels have a more lively interest, for they have been made gay with deep borders of perennials along three sides. The fourth side in each case is in effect a flower border, for it is marked by a retaining wall of rubble masonry whose crevices are filled with rock plants. These two intermediate gardens, lying between the lower turf garden and the paved terrace at the house, are so similar in design that variety must be provided by means of a difference in color schemes.

Two lateral paths provide access to the gardens from the steps at either end of the terrace. The steps at each of the two drops in grade are built of brick to give a nice contrast to the stone of the walls. Two plots have been laid out at the south end of each intermediate garden for small vegetables and flowers for cutting.

An interesting and effective type of enclosure has been given the garage court by using pleached Lindens. The trees are planted fairly close together and then sheared to give the appearance of a clipped hedge whose branches begin about five feet from the ground.

*The plan illustrates the plot arrangement, which drops first from the street to the front lawn, then to the terrace, and thence through three garden levels*

# A  HOUSE  OF  SUNNY  ARCHITECTURE

*Designed for California and the South*
*by  Johnson,  Kaufmann  &  Coate*

FOR the Coast or the South it would be difficult to find a house more suited than this one to such a situation. At the same time it has features of design and plan which might with perfect ease and safety be adapted to houses of Italian or Spanish small-house architecture in the North.

The idea here has been to leave as much as possible to simplicity. From that rare quality much of the effectiveness of the house has come. A great deal more is shown of the beautiful art of building than of "architecture". You feel in the house, as well as in its particular style, the real existence of walls and roofs, handled skilfully, of course, and with an eye to their loveliness, but especially you feel that they are distinctly walls and roofs, however gracefully their forms compose in the mass. This is characteristic of such an architecture as this which holds closely to the traditions of a primitive period. The style of the house is several centuries old, perhaps, but it has always marked the outposts of civilization (in Northern Mexico and our Southwest and on the lower coast of California) and so has until even now kept its frontier flavor.

While this house has all the sophistication that goes with a modern building conscious of its beauty, it retains the delightful naïvete of the adobe houses which were its prototypes. Planned to contain all the conveniences of present-day living it manages very subtly indeed to appear casual.

With that sort of personality the house does not require any definite formality; in fact, strict formality would make restless the building's easy nature and put restrictions on its rambling charm.

One might very readily imagine this house having been built from time to time as the need arose for greater room. It might gradually have spread itself out, beginning with the central main structure which lies across the slope and increasing itself at various times with the additions that are the living room and service wing. This semblance of a gradual growth not only gives the house a fine picturesque quality, but suggests an actual method for its construction if it were desired to let the house grow with the requirements of the occupants.

This house lies lengthwise on its forward sloping lot, hugs the ground and follows its rising levels. The exterior is plastered in smooth white plaster with soft edges at the corners and openings. Instead of using a straight-edge in truing up the surfaces of the walls a texture, as of old work, is given them with the trowel. The roof is laid with hand-made, mission-type, red tiles, set quite at random both as to horizontal and vertical lines and with a very uneven line along the eaves. This effect is obtained by using many broken tiles and by doubling up the layers here and there, all of which produces a very interesting shadow upon the white plaster wall below.

Most of the architectural interest is concentrated here about the patio which becomes, in effect, an outdoor living room. A balcony on the second floor level runs along one side and steps descend into the patio through an intermediate terrace. The patio itself lies on a level halfway between that of the terrace, which leads into the entrance hallway, and the main entrance gateway in the street wall. Its paths are paved so that it can be used at all times and its beds are filled with plants which flourish in flower or foliage throughout the year.

As may be seen from the elevations and plans on the next page the house rises to a two story height over only a comparatively small section. In the case of the living room, which is in a one story wing, the wooden timbers of the roof are left exposed inside. By keeping the house long and rather narrow it has been possible to get cross ventilation in most of the rooms of the first floor. A pleasant feature of the service section on this floor is the semi-enclosed porch which is used as a laundry and outside storage space. A bedroom and bath occupy a kind of eddy in the stream of the household which flows between the dining room-service wing and the entrance hall and living room; yet the passageways have been so cleverly arranged that its presence is unnoticeable. It is often desirable to have such an apartment as this on the living floor; and to have it provided so completely and with such generosity if

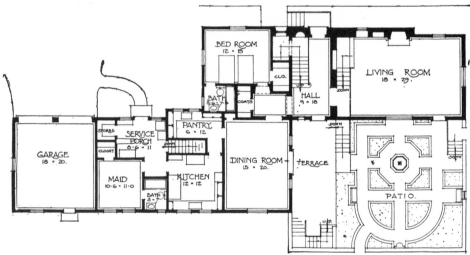

*This house, for California or Florida, with its unmistakable origin, its soft lines and simple surfaces, lies lengthwise on its lot, so that from the south side elevation immediately above one gets the impression of considerable size, whereas the rear elevation at the top of the page shows that the house is really quite small*

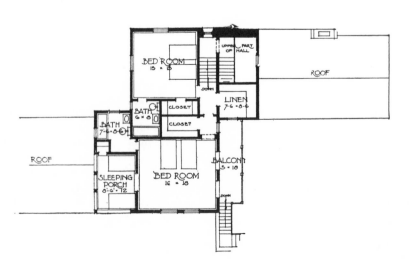

*There is no use envying the things which go with the loose, recumbent houses of the Coast; they belong—balconies and outside stairways and all—to that balmy climate; and such plans as these, which allow one's living so close to outdoors, would need some slight revision for a place elsewhere, though they are crowded with clever suggestions as they stand*

*All the charm to be found in the smaller Spanish and Italian houses has been put into this one, with its white plaster walls and its red roof of rough, hand-made Mission tiles*

*In this case the lot slopes upward from the street front, so that inside one finds the living room at a lower level than that of the first floor which lies beyond towards the rear*

space is as unusual as it is welcome.

The dining room is well-sized and of splendid proportions. Two windows and a French door make it an almost integral part of the terrace. The hallway makes a direct connection, and a delightful one, between the doorway on the drive and this terrace overlooking the patio. A low balcony in the living room comes off the hallway on the level of the latter and a half-dozen steps descend to the living room floor. This following of the grades of the grounds outside by the floor levels of the interior gives the house inside a connection with the site as close as that afforded by the ridges that rise with the slope.

Upstairs there are two large bedrooms, each with its bath and commodious closets, and one with its sleeping porch. Off the hallway between the two rooms opens the balcony from which an outside staircase descends to the terrace and thence to the patio.

A feature that every good housewife will appreciate is the generous size of the linen room. This is lighted by a window on the balcony. If one desired, this room could be finished in cedar for a clothes storage space and one of the long closets equipped with linen shelves.

It will be noted that, as in the previous house, the garage is made an integral part of the composition, containing on its end the long low roof line of the living room wing. The attached garage is a necessity in the well designed house that has limited grounds, for it is practically impossible to make a detached building without taking precious space that might otherwise be devoted to lawn and garden. In the case of this garage there is no necessity for a door from the house, although one could be cut through the service porch.

*Simplicity and an absence of all un-
necessary furniture are character-
istics of Spanish interiors. This austerity is more than offset by brilliant
wall hangings, beautiful carving
and intricate wrought iron work*

*The lamps used in the living room
above are made of Spanish pottery
jars in vivid blue, yellow, copper
and black. The parchment shades are
copper colored with decorations in
blue and yellow at the top and bottom*

FINDING suitable furniture for this
house was a comparatively simple matter,
for the wide interest in Spanish decoration
today has resulted in some remarkably good
reproductions of Spanish furniture of the
16th and 17th Centuries. While it was
thought advisable to keep pretty much to
Spanish types in this house on account of
the character of the architecture, there was
no strict adherence to period,
and in several instances furniture of other countries was
introduced. Some of the
pieces in the living room such
as the two tables and desk are
frankly Spanish in design,
but the arm chair by the window is Italian, the gilt mirror
over the table at the left of
the stairway Venetian, and
the comfortable overstuffed
sofa and chair decidedly
modern. The Italian pieces,
however, are quite in character with the other furniture and the introduction of
an overstuffed sofa and chair

was a concession to modern ideas of comfort.

The sofa and long table were placed in
front of the fireplace as this seemed the
most logical spot for them, and the smaller
pieces such as the three-foot table, desk and
arm chair in the available wall spaces. This
arrangement gives a sense of space and although the room may look a trifle bare and
under-furnished, there is in
reality sufficient furniture.
Spanish interiors are char-
acterized by a look of bareness, almost of austerity, the
people of that country pre-
ferring to rely for their decorative effects on brilliant
wall hangings, richly carved
doors and ceilings, lace-like
wrought iron work and colored tiles.

*The furniture is arranged
so as to give a sense of
space. By placing most of
the pieces near the wall
the center of the room is
left free*

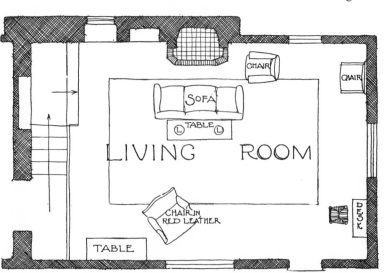

*A green and gold printed cotton material, an excellent reproduction of old damask, is used to make the wall hanging. It is bound with gold galloon*

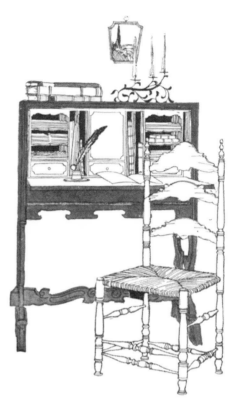

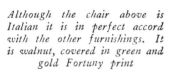

*Although the chair above is Italian it is in perfect accord with the other furnishings. It is walnut, covered in green and gold Fortuny print*

*A small walnut desk, Spanish in design, is placed at the right of the large window. The ladder back chair of brown mahogany has a rush seat*

*The material used for the wall hanging and chair covering is a cotton fabric printed in green and gold. It looks remarkably like old damask. Such hangings relieve the barren aspect of the rough plastered walls found in Spanish houses*

The ground is green, the cartouches black and white outlined by gold scrolls and the flowers surrounding these motifs copper, mauve, blue, pink and red. It is an enchanting fabric and quite compensates for the bare walls and lack of decorative objects. A room of this kind with windows usually opening on to a patio or garden does

*The material used for the window hangings in this room is a hand-blocked linen with a green ground and a scene of a Spanish cavalier and his lady in black and white, outlined with gold scrolls and surrounded by a flower design in vivid colors*

The walls are plaster, slightly rough in texture and tinted a deep pinkish cream tone. The woodwork, what there is of it, and the exposed beam ceiling and floor are stained very dark. This contrast of light and shade, further emphasized by the wrought iron railing on the stairway is one of the most attractive features of the room.

The cool expanse of plaster walls makes an effective background for the vivid fabric of the curtains—a heavy hand-blocked linen, sixty inches wide. This pattern with its sweeping scrolls, interesting cartouches depicting a Spanish cavalier and his lady, and graceful clusters of flowers is typically Spanish in coloring.

not need another set of curtains, but if these are deemed necessary there is a sunfast changeable copper and gold gauze that would repeat the tones of the overhangings.

The color scheme of green, gold and copper has been followed in the coverings of the furniture. The sofa is done in a heavy cotton sunfast material in a wide green and copper stripe and the overstuffed chair beside it in a deep gold colored ribbed fabric, also sunfast. The wall-hanging back of the table by the stairway, which so effectively silhouettes a graceful gilded Venetian mirror, is a printed cotton that looks remarkably like old damask, available at a fraction of the cost.

*The Kashmir goat's hair rug in fantastic design and colors can be used for a hanging either over the chest pictured above, or a mirror can be substituted, as shown on page 27*

*One end of the room has a china cupboard with doors, a chest, and the door leading to the hallway painted grayish blue. Walls are painted bright gray blue and antiqued*

*The rug in the Spanish dining room is a modern worsted Wilton reproducing a 17th Century Persian, with faded tones of red, yellow and blue on a deep blue ground*

*Curtains are of this printed cotton cloth of a deep yellow ground with a rose red damask pattern. It is a soft, pliable fabric with the appearance of old brocade*

THE color scheme of the dining room is red, white and blue. The plaster walls are painted a rather bright gray blue and antiqued. This color is more interesting than the ordinary cream plaster wall and gives the room a rich, dignified background. The woodwork is painted a darker shade and glazed.

In striking contrast to this soft, restful tone is the color of the curtain—a printed cotton cloth with the luminous quality of old damask. It has a deep yellow ground, almost gold color, and a design in warm rose red. It is a soft, pliable material that from a distance looks remarkably like old hand loomed brocade. The curtains are hung with loops on a wrought iron rod. If under curtains are desired, heavy coarse net might be dyed the color of the walls and bound in red.

It would be interesting to use plain white Italian pottery in this room—Deruta and Bassano ware. The note of white would be a charming contrast to the blue walls and rose red curtains, and in place of Italian linen, a piece of deep red brocade might be

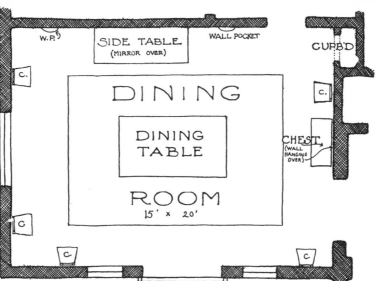

The floor plan shows the disposition of the furniture, the doors and windows. The door at the bottom leads to the terrace. The window to the left is pictured below. The door on the right leads to the pantry and the door above to the hallway

While plain white Italian pottery could be used for table service, the china in the cupboard might be of more colorful pattern. The interior of this cupboard may be painted bright blue to make it a color accent

In the perspective above is shown the pantry side of the dining room, with its serving table and wall pockets of wrought iron. Both tables are Spanish reproductions. On the floor is a Wilton Persian rug

W. P.    SIDE TABLE
(MIRROR OVER)    WALL POCKET    CURB'D

C.

DINING

DINING
TABLE    C.

CHEST.
(WALL
HANGING
OVER)

ROOM
15' x 20'

C

C

used as runner on the dining table.

The furniture is mostly walnut, excellent reproductions of Spanish pieces of the early 17th Century. The dining table has the characteristic iron underbracing of the period, and there is a bit of interesting carving on the backs of the chairs. The oak chest at the far end of the room is a copy of an English piece. Above this is an interesting hanging made of felted goat's hair, with brilliant embroidery in tan, brown, red, blue and yellow on a natural colored

ground. It is really a rug, made in the city of Shrinigar in Kashmir. On account of its fantastic, colorful design it makes an effective and unusual hanging for an interior of this kind. A mirror can be substituted for this hanging.

The rug in this room is a worsted Wilton, a very good reproduction of a 17th Century Persian rug. The ground is deep blue, darker than the walls, and the graceful floral and scroll design is in soft, faded tones of red, yellow and blue, the main notes of the room.

*Because the long windows in the room above disclose a lovely view of balcony and patio, only one set of hangings was used. These are of green printed linen*

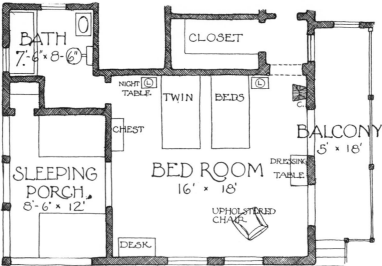

*The plan at the left shows a convenient arrangement of furniture. If preferred, the desk may be placed beside one bed instead of the night table.*

THE master's bedroom combines modern ideas of comfort with the picturesque aspect of Spanish interiors of the 16th and 17th Centuries. While using modern furniture Spanish in line or feeling, an effort was made in decorating this room to overcome the look of austerity and bareness characteristic of the majority of Spanish interiors as found in the original.

In the first place the room glows with color. The warm pinkish orange tone of the plaster walls was suggested by the block printed linen of the hangings. This has a soft green ground and a lovely sprawling design—graceful scrolls, birds and flowers—in henna, mauve, orange, yellow and blue. This material makes the long curtains and the wall hanging behind the beds.

By using a wall hanging, the bare expanse of plaster walls was successfully relieved, while the vari-colored fabric, so interesting a color contrast to the pinkish orange walls, brings the necessary note of design to this portion of the room and, in addition, makes an interesting and colorful background for the graceful curved headboards of the beds.

Much of the picturesque, colorful look of early Spanish interiors is due to the use of brilliant wall hangings. Practically every material was used—painted canvas, tapestry, brocade, damask, velvet, leather, gilded and ornamented with polychrome work, linen and printed cloths of all kinds. These more than atoned for the austerity of the plaster walls and scarcity of furniture. In the living room of this house a wall hanging in green and gold was used on the wall opposite the fireplace. This wall hanging of printed linen is a feature of the bedroom.

Other color notes in the room are provided by the covering of the overstuffed chair—a linen with a henna ground and a narrow stripe in yellow, green and black—and by the material on the seat of the straight chair, a heavy basket weave cotton cloth in mauve and blue. The bedspreads are made of a mercerized strié material, strongly resembling taffeta, in soft green, the tone of the background of the printed linen, piped with orange. If under curtains are used they might be of heavy coarse net

*A graceful walnut bed, with a beautiful curved and shaped head board, is silhouetted by a wall hanging of the same printed linen as the curtains. The desk here is suggested as an alternative for one night table*

*On a sturdy oak night table is a simple and effective lamp made of a Spanish pottery jar in dull, soft green. The parchment shade is decorated with narrow green and black lines*

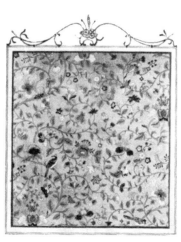

*The material used in this bedroom for both curtains and wall hanging is a block printed linen with a soft green ground and a graceful scroll and flower pattern in red, henna, mauve, yellow and blue*

*At the right of the door leading to the sleeping porch (see plan on opposite page) is this sturdy chest of beech, stained a dark walnut. The lighting fixtures are wrought iron*

in either gold color or the tone of the walls.

The beds because of the excellence of their design form the most interesting group in the room. They are walnut stained very dark and antiqued. The graceful curved headboards are brought into prominence by the wall hanging of printed linen behind, from which the color of the bedspreads was taken.

The night table is oak with a tray top and convenient drawer. If preferred, a small Spanish desk may be placed by the side of one bed in place of another night table.

This arrangement is shown in the sketch at the top of page 28. The lamp on the small bedside table is a Spanish pottery jar in dull soft green, with a simple parchment shade painted orange with green and black lines, repeating the main color of the curtains. The straight chairs in this room are comfortable and a bit unusual in design. The one in the group with the desk is Italian but quite in keeping with the rest of the furnishings. The frame is beech, stained dark walnut color, and the back and seat are covered in a durable basket weave material in dull blue and mauve. The other straight chair, which is shown at the left of the window in the sketch at the top of page 28, is a picturesque ladder back model with a rush seat.

Both the chest of drawers and the dressing table are beech, stained a dark walnut shade and antiqued to give the mellow look of old furniture. The dressing table is an old interesting model with slender iron underbracing and a graceful triple standing mirror. The wrought iron note is found again in the lighting fixtures—single light wall brackets in a graceful design of leaves. If more light is needed a pair of tall iron candlesticks might be used on the dressing table.

The rug here is wool Wilton in dark taupe color. It has an all-over pattern.

*Outside the dining room is a broad terrace overlooking the sunny patio. This is simply furnished with wicker and wrought iron pieces. Very gay is the effect produced by a row of colorful potted plants*

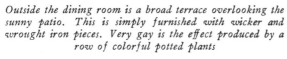

*At one end of the terrace is a group of interesting wrought iron furniture. The table has a marbleized top and the chair a cane seat and back*

A DELIGHTFUL feature of this Spanish house is the wide, paved terrace overlooking the sunny patio. This is used as an outdoor living room and is simply furnished with wicker and wrought iron pieces. At one end is a stairway to a balcony on the second floor level, and at the other a short flight of steps leads to the paved paths of the patio.

A group of iron furniture consisting of a graceful table and two chairs occupies one end of the terrace. The table has a wrought iron base and an attractive marbleized top, while the chairs, in an unusually smart design, are a combination of iron and cane. An effective note here would be cushions covered in colored oilcloth. Over the table hangs a graceful, wrought iron wall bracket filled with trailing plants.

At the other end of the terrace is a comfortable arm chair made of Swiss willow, enameled a soft green. If more chairs are needed, Chinese rattan furniture, especially

the kind ornamented with black motifs, might be used, as it is both decorative and practical.

A row of plants in attractively shaped pots completes the furnishings of this sunny, out-door living room. The large jars at the end and in the center are intended for such plants as Palms, Aspidistras, Hydrangeas and Bay trees. They are made of terra cotta in a light, stone gray.

The smaller plants are in the regulation terra cotta colored earthenware flower pots, which have a decorative quality often overlooked.

THE extra bedroom in this house has been furnished as a guest room. In contrast to the main bedroom with its mixture of picturesque Spanish and Italian pieces is the early American character of this room created mainly by the furniture— good reproductions of early styles in an interesting combination of maple and mahogany. The bed, bureau, mirror, night tables and secretary are in this combination of woods and in addition there is a small chest of drawers and low table in walnut. The only other piece of furniture is a small wing chair covered in the same material as the bedspread.

This is a gay striped chintz copied from an old Portuguese design. It has wide bright blue and white stripes and flowers in brilliant red, with here and there a note

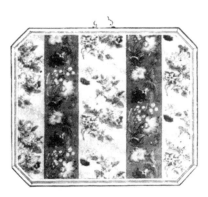

*The plan at the right shows a convenient arrangement of furniture in a bedroom absolutely square. The secretary and bureau on either side of the window balance the bed and night tables*

*This chintz copied from an old Portuguese design has wide blue and white stripes and flowers in brilliant red*

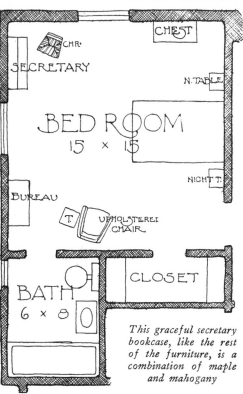

*Grayish white plaster walls and a striking striped chintz in blue and red contrast pleasingly with the mellow tones of maple and mahogany. The curtains are plain blue glazed chintz*

*This graceful secretary bookcase, like the rest of the furniture, is a combination of maple and mahogany*

of yellow and green. The bright blue of this fabric is so effective with maple furniture that it has been repeated in the curtains. These are blue glazed chintz bound in red. Under curtains of heavy, cream colored net are also edged with red. The rug is sand colored.

A practical as well as decorative feature of this room is the commodious secretary bookcase in one corner between the windows.

On the opposite side of the room are a small wing chair, covered in the striped chintz, and a low walnut table. The lamp (not shown in the sketch) is a copy of an early American glass lamp, amber colored.

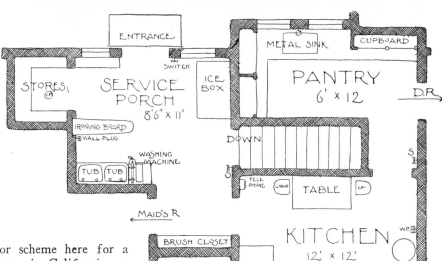

*A color scheme of green and white gives the kitchen in this California house brightness and coolness. The stove is hooded for better ventilation*

*The plan is particularly interesting because the kitchen unit includes a semi-enclosed service porch which houses the laundry, stores closet and refrigerator*

THE color scheme here for a sunny home in California, or elsewhere, is effective in green and white. The curtains can be of linen in natural color bound in green, or green linen.

The floor here is of green and white rubber or linoleum tile—cool and refreshing.

This layout contains the kitchen, pantry, and service porch in which is the laundry equipment. This service porch is semi-enclosed and can be shut up completely whenever necessary. But the worker has the comfort of working in the fresh air, when the weather is good.

The kitchen cabinets and cupboards are of the finest manufacture and are securely installed. Here, though, if you require other cabinets, the metal or wood units, for example, they can be substituted for what is seen in this sketch.

The central electric light gives ample light at night, fortified by the sink light.

The gas range is of magnificent proportions, hooded to take care of rising vapors and fumes. The range can be smooth or spider topped.

The pantry has a metal sink to reduce the possibility of breaking fine china. There is a house phone situated in the kitchen so that the maids can get the orders from the mistress's boudoir without extra runs.

On the way to the service department you will see the brush and broom closets.

These too, can be built in or purchased in whatever shape and dimensions needed.

In this service porch near the outside entry you will see the refrigerator, easy of access for the iceman and not so far as it looks from the kitchen.

Here is the washing machine with its electric motor, and the covered tubs which can be used as tables.

This laundry is well aired. The ironing board lies flat against the wall when not in use, and the washing machine is attached to the plumbing and can be used without tubs if wringerless. Use the nearer end of the tub for wringing operations if you have a washer with wringer, this will conserve footsteps. A wall plug for the iron is conveniently located, and there are other switches on the porch.

The store closet here will be convenient. In other houses it is better on account of the plans to have this closet in the cellar.

*The patio, which in this case is the principal garden, is surrounded by a seven-foot wall plastered to harmonize with the house, of which it is an integral part. This tiled fountain is set against the wall opposite the living room*

WHILE the lower coast of California, and Florida, with their balmy subtropical weather, were the climates for which this house was intended, it would be a mistake to suppose that it could be adapted to none but those tender latitudes. Actually, it is a hardy architectural type, fit for any part of the country. The same might be said of its garden. The plants would have to suit the habits of the seasons, wherever the garden were made, but the framework and the character of its design are not, for any practical purposes, bound down to a particular locality.

The house and the garden illustrate the kind of architecture and landscape design which has been made especially popular in California because of its derivation from Mediterranean sources, where the sun, sea and sky have a similar effect upon the art of building. But apart from the matter of style, the house and its garden scheme show how admirably the problem of a sloping site may be solved. It is an unusual sort of solution, for generally when a slope exists the house is set across it. Here the house runs with the slope, and, rather than protrude at the lower end and bury itself in the hill at the upper, it rises with the incline; each section being put on a slightly higher level as the house works toward the rear of the plot.

Three different parts of the house connect with the grounds at the places where their levels coincide. The patio is the most important of these, and it lies on the living room level. The driveway entrance and the terrace are at the next higher level, and the garage court at the highest. The ground is still higher back of the garage, where a vegetable garden has been made to be reached by steps and a path from a service door.

The grounds as a whole have been very simply handled: a driveway leads straight from the street to the garage, and connecting paths at various places do their work as directly and unostentatiously as possible. The planting, other than that of the patio and vegetable garden, is merely an arrangement of shrubbery about the base of the building. Six large Eucalyptus trees formed the only existing growth on the plot.

*This drawing tells the story of the house and its site. The former has been designed to fit the rising slope of the latter, and in following the grade up from the high-way in front the house has fallen into a most attractive series of levels. On the lowest lies the patio. Johnson, Kaufmann & Coate, architects. Drawn by Chester B. Price*

The paths of the patio have been paved with flagstones and lined with edgings of Dwarf Box. The small central beds are filled for the most part with low-growing annuals to keep a rather flat effect over the middle portion—an effect which gives emphasis to the greater bulk and height in the larger outside borders where shrubs and very small trees are used towards the background. The plants here are given numerals corresponding to their positions on the plan.

## PLANT LIST

| (1) | *Abelia grandiflora* | Glossy Abelia |
| | *Cotoneaster horizontalis* | Rock Cotoneaster |
| | *Hypericum moserianum* | Gold flower |
| (2) | *Abelia grandiflora* | Glossy Abelia |
| | *Symphoricarpos racemosus* | Snowberry |
| | *Kerria japonica* | Kerria |
| | *Cotoneaster horizontalis* | Rock Cotoneaster |
| (3) | *Magnolia* | Magnolia |
| (4) | *Berberis thunbergi* | Japanese Barberry |
| | *Berberis thunbergi* | Japanese Barberry |
| (5) | *Cotoneaster horizontalis* | Rock Cotoneaster |
| (6) | *Crataegus cordata* | Washington Thorn |

| (7) | *Crataegus cordata* | Washington Thorn |
| (8) | *Euonymous japonicus* | Evergreen Bittersweet |
| (9) | *Euonymous japonicus* | Evergreen Bittersweet |
| (10) | *Euonymous japonicus* | Evergreen Bittersweet |
| | *Berberis thunbergi* | Japanese Barberry |
| (11) | *Kerria japonica* | Kerria |
| | *Abelia grandiflora* | Glossy Abelia |
| | *Azalea nudica* | Indian Azalea |
| (12) | *Berberis thunbergi* | Japanese Barberry |
| (13) | *Berberis thunbergi* | Japanese Barberry |
| (14-25) | | |
| | *Coreopsis tinctoria* | Tickseed |

| | *Gallardia grandiflora* | Blanket Flower |
| | *Lilium Henryi* | Yellow Lily |
| | *Phlox drummondi* | Drummond Phlox |
| | *Viola* vars. | Horned Violets in varie |
| | *Yucca filamentosa* | Adam's Needle |
| | Petunias | |
| | Gladioli | |
| | Zinnias | |
| | *Papaver orientalis* | Oriental Poppy |
| | *Gypsophila paniculata* | Baby's Breath |
| (26) | *Ligustrum ovalifolium* | California Privet |
| (27) | *Ligustrum ovalifolium* | California Privet |

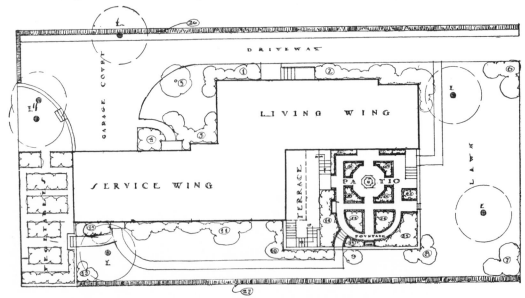

*The plan shows how the garden treatment is concentrated in the patio; elsewhere the aim is merely to provide a setting for the house. The numerals refer to plants named in the text*

# A HOUSE IN THE ENGLISH MANNER

*Half-Timber, Stucco and Stone,*
*Designed by Howell & Thomas*

ONE of the finest qualities in the architecture of this house is the mellowness it is able to achieve through the use of varied materials. Its lines, both in plan and elevation, have a pleasing lack of rigidity; its gables and corners falling from every angle into delightful compositions. It is less consciously picturesque than most houses done in the style that has come to be known as the English cottage, but the lack of that trait may be traced to its Tudor tendencies. The Tudor style, for all its apparent informality, had dignity. That dignity has been combined in this house with the simple cottage manner. The result is an easy, unaffected building, human and comfortable. The materials of which the house is built fit nicely into the mood of the mellow architecture. Stone, stucco and timber have a natural affinity for each other, and this is particularly true here where a warm soft tone pervades each one. The stucco is tan, the timber a natural weathered color, and the stone a range of brown to blue with generously pointed joints in cement the color of the stucco. It would be a pity in a house so quiet in manner to set one material playing against another by giving them sharply contrasting colors. One of its great charms lies in the fact that its color effects are subtle. Not immediately do you feel that it is composed of a variety of materials. It is the sort of house which, like a sensible person, ages

gracefully. That part of the first story wall which surrounds the living room wing is built up of whatever native stone the locality happens to afford. Elsewhere the walls are of stucco over either tile or frame. These stuccoed surfaces are broken by two stone chimneys and by beams of weather stained timbers that enter actually into the structure of the building. The roof might be laid in slates, flat tiles or colored shingles.

Perfect regularity and symmetry must necessarily be avoided in a house of this type. Its charm lies in other directions. But what there must be, and what most certainly exist here, are splendid proportions among the various parts and a fine balance in the arrangements of windows and doorways. Each face of the house is a nicely studied composition, and this is not merely superficial; for the windows and doors are also placed where they are in order to fit the interior arrangement.

The entrance porch, which is set under one corner of the front gable, is built up of heavy oak posts and braces, and the two faces of the house within this semi-enclosed space are half-timbered. A sturdy balustrade in the same wood fills in the two panels between the columns on the side. A less robust treatment of such an inset porch as this would make the entrance seem structurally weak, even though it were not actually so. Here the timbers of the porch ap-

pear just as capable of supporting their section of the upper story of the gable as the adjoining masonry seems able to uphold the balance. And this is a really much more important point than one might think, for any sign of weakness at a place where strength is necessary is unconsciously caught by the eye, and whether or not one is aware of the discrepancy the effect is restless and disturbing.

The English character of the house is emphasized by the use throughout of casements set in timbered frames. Some of the windows are diamond-paned, the others rectangular in their leaded pattern. Variety in the fenestration is furthered by the marked difference in size and shape of the window openings. No two sets of windows are obviously similar, yet there is a nice relationship between them, as one may judge from the elevations.

Each side of the house is quite unlike every other, yet they all merge harmoniously. The front gable, for instance, is rather dignified, while the double one facing the garage is almost impertinent. The roof line there resembles a great M: a scheme of construction whose shape is made more unusual by the down spout that divides the façade.

The garage is extremely unobtrusive. Its flat roof is no higher than is absolutely necessary and a sharp line along its front is avoided by the deep arbor which over-

The garden elevation above and the east side elevation below it carry out with fine consistency the particular English cottage style which finds its best adaptation in this country in houses of stone and stucco. The straightforward design of this Howell & Thomas house, its restraint, and its irregular loveliness, give it great distinction

The W-shaped first floor plan on the left hand side of the page shows an extremely interesting room arrangement made possible by this clever devising: a living room with light on four sides, a well connected garage, and, upstairs, large, light bedrooms, and many closets conveniently placed

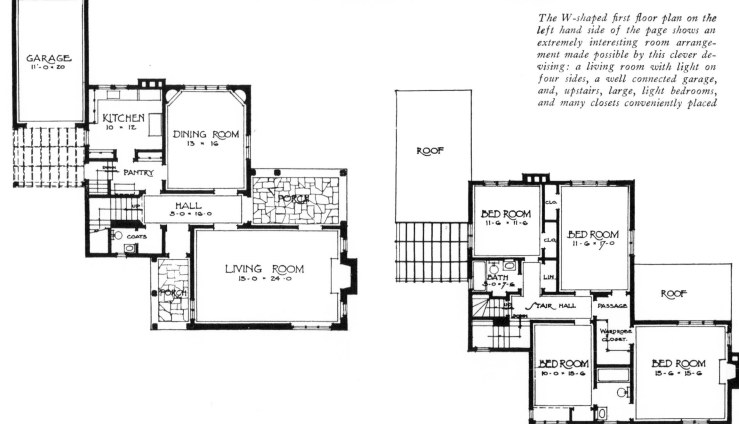

*Stone, stucco and timber are the materials of this gracefully gabled house whose English air is emphasized by the use of diamond-pane casements and sturdy beams at the entrance*

*The plot for this house is level, but its garden side faces the sunless north, so the building has been given a sun-trap plan to catch all possible light from other directions*

hangs the double-doored entrance. This arbor provides protection when entering or leaving a car, or going to or from the garage, as it also covers the service doorway leading through the pantry into the main hallway.

In studying the floor plans it must be remembered that the garden side of the house faces north. From that direction there is but seldom any direct sunlight, so the room arrangement had to be devised to overcome that difficulty and yet make as much use as possible of that most private and important side. This was done by giving the plan a W-shape.

The living room is large and is lighted from all sides. From it French windows lead out on to the garden porch, while a balancing doorway leads into the hallway separating it from the dining room. This hallway is so arranged that one may pass from any room to the staircase without going through another room, and while the service is an integral part of the house, circulation among its various rooms may be accomplished without the slightest inconvenience. For rainy weather there is a doorway from the hall, through the pantry, to the garage.

Upstairs three large bedrooms and one small one have been provided, with two baths and adequate closet space.

A half-timbered house of this English cottage type is adaptable to almost any section of the country, save those regions that are pronouncedly Spanish. It is a house that would be dignified by an even larger lot than is designed here, and would serve for a small country house. It can also be visualized as gracing a suburban street, because it is a type of house that is worth the investment in a restricted locality. One could live in it easily and be proud of its possession.

*The small paned leaded glass windows set in plaster recesses, the leaded glass windows set in oak frames, the oak cornice, baseboard and flooring are noteworthy features of this room*

*Heavy jute fabric printed in Jacobean design in rich reds, yellows, blues and greens on a natural colored background. This material makes the curtains and chair coverings*

THE decoration of the English living room—the rough plaster walls, oak furniture and strongly colored fabrics—was inspired by the sturdy interiors of 16th and 17th Century England. This type of decoration is peculiarly well adapted to modern living conditions as it is essentially comfortable and easy to live with. The colors are strong and direct, the designs of the fabrics varied and interesting and the furniture substantial and commodious.

The walls here are of sand finished plaster which has been glazed with sepia to give it a soft look of age. This type of wall makes an excellent background for colorful draperies and oak furniture, and in addition contrasts pleasingly with the dark trim and floor characteristic of interiors of this kind. The woodwork in this case—the cornice, baseboards and window trim—is of oak, antiqued and waxed. The ceiling is a lighter tone than the plaster walls and the floor is stained dark brown and waxed. The mantel is antiqued oak with a decorative carved molding and the fireplace is bordered on either side with dull, yellowish stone blocks. An interesting fire back with a heavily embossed design characteristic of the period has been used, and the andirons have graceful pierced discs of antique brass.

A room of this kind with plain plaster walls needs colorful hangings and upholstery. The fabric chosen for the curtains and to cover the roomy arm chair is a heavy jute fabric printed in an authentic Jacobean design in reds, yellows, greens and blues, on a natural colored background. Small side chairs

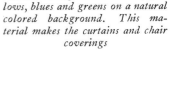

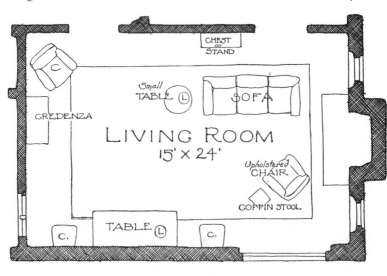

CHEST on STAND

Small TABLE (L)

SOFA

CREDENZA

C.

LIVING ROOM
15' X 24'

Upholstered CHAIR

COFFIN STOOL

C.    TABLE (L)    C.

*The placing of the furniture was influenced by deference to wall space, lighting facilities and ease and sociability of living*

*The carved oak chest at the left is mounted on a turned oak trestle. The wood has been antiqued and has a wax finish. This could be converted into a radio cabinet*

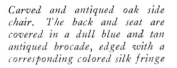

*Carved and antiqued oak side chair. The back and seat are covered in a dull blue and tan antiqued brocade, edged with a corresponding colored silk fringe*

*Italian credenza of walnut in antique finish. The wooden handles are elaborately turned, as are the heavy moldings on the base and the panels on the front and sides*

of oak are covered with a dull blue brocade and the couch is upholstered in a crimson sunfast fabric with loose slip cushions covered in the same material as the curtains. An interesting variation from the customary curtain treatment is accomplished by having the hangings at the large window of the printed material and the curtains at the two small recessed windows on either side of the fireplace of red sunfast gauze. The rug here is made of a wide-loom carpeting in tête de nègre color.

The furniture here is a mixture of oak and walnut in antique finish. A large table for lamps, books, magazines, etc. is placed in one long wall space with a chair on either side. This makes a nice grouping, slightly formal in appearance. The fireplace group consists of a comfortable overstuffed chair with a reading lamp beside it and a small stool for a few books and smoking things, and a commodious sofa opposite. At one end of this stands an oval table, shown in the plan of the room but not in the drawing. At the far end opposite the fireplace is an Italian credenza in walnut with an overstuffed chair beside it, and on the

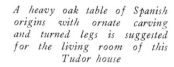

*The small occasional table above is oak with turned legs and stretchers. The finish is a dark antique brown. Size of top 20 inches by 32 inches*

*A heavy oak table of Spanish origins with ornate carving and turned legs is suggested for the living room of this Tudor house*

side wall opposite the long table is a carved chest mounted on an oak trestle.

The lighting fixtures in this room are of silver plated oxidized metal in a graceful shell design. These have two-inch candle sockets wired for electricity. These electric candles may be taken out and two inch beeswax candles substituted if one prefers a more mellow lighting. In addition to these wall brackets, wrought iron Italian candlesticks standing five feet high are placed at either side of the fireplace. These also are intended to hold two-inch candles. The lamp beside the overstuffed chair is also of wrought iron. This has a parchment shade in natural color, decorated with bands in red and blue to carry out the colors of the curtains.

A pair of old Persian oil jars in vivid blue are used for the lamps on the large table. These have shades of parchment painted copper color with red and blue bands at the top and bottom.

Pewter, brass and bits of Chinese pottery are attractive accessories in a room of this kind. A pair of old brass candlesticks is used on the mantel.

*Authentic copies of a Welsh dresser and an English chair are in natural colored oak with an antique finish. Wrought iron sconces can be used for electricity or for beeswax candles*

*Scenes of rural English country life are depicted in deep shades of blue on a white ground, in this china for the house whose architecture is of Tudor tendencies*

*Rich blues and tans, on a crimson ground, combine in a small all-over pattern to make this an ideal rug for an English type of dining room*

*The hand-blocked 36 inch curtain linen copies an old tapestry on which, against preposterous hills, are sport dogs and deer. Deep blues, greens, reds and tans*

IN PLANNING the decoration of the dining room an effort was made to bring charm and interest into this interior without detracting from its appearance of sturdy simplicity. The structural details, the straight-forward furniture and the rich coloring of curtains and rug create a decorative as well as extremely livable room.

Wide beamed oak flooring is stained a dark brown and finished with a dull gloss varnish which is kept in good condition by frequent rubbing with floor polish. The danger of slipping is thus done away with while the varnish finish in no way detracts from the appearance of the floor. The woodwork—trim, baseboard, cornice and paneling—is natural colored oak rubbed with sepia and waxed. The walls and ceiling are of hand finished plaster that has been rubbed with a dull gloss varnish.

An interesting architectural feature of this room is the paneling around the windows at one end and the built-in china cupboards. The shelves and insides of these are painted bright red—a cheerful note in an interior of this kind and particularly effective in contrast to the plaster walls and oak woodwork.

The curtains here are of heavy handblocked linen—a copy of the quaint old tapestries that hung in every well-regulated Jacobean home of ample means. It has a deep blue ground and an amusing design of hills, dogs and deer in green, reds and tans. The curtains are hung with traverse fixtures on rods which are concealed in grooves in the wooden framework. No valances or glass curtains are necessary in a room of this type, and, moreover, they would detract from the structural beauty of the window and its framework. An interesting bit of design and color is provided by the Turkish rug which has a warm red ground on which a small all-over pattern is carried out in blues, gold and tan.

The Welsh dresser, chairs and table are reproductions of old English pieces in natural colored oak in dull, antique finish. The chairs have flat pads covered in red jaspé sunfast fabric attached to them with self colored cords.

For lighting fixtures a simple design in wrought iron in dull rust finish was selected—a copy of an old English wall bracket. These may be used as electric candles, or should a more mellow light be preferred, a two-inch beeswax candle can be used. At meal times pewter or brass candle sticks should be used on the table.

*Built-in corner cupboards simplify to a great extent the furnishing, and give the semblance of a deep bay to the farther end of the room. This affords fine light for the day-time meals*

*Furniture in this dining room is arranged with consideration for practicability and ease of service. Interest is produced by richness of coloring in carpet, china and curtains*

It will be seen that the curtains and rug with their Oriental richness of color make up for the neutral tones of the woodwork and furniture. Additional color interest is provided by the china selected for this room. This is a pottery set depicting rural English scenes in deep blues on a white ground. This note of bright blue is an effective contrast to the red in the room and particularly attractive with oak. If preferred, blue and white Canton china might be used here, or peasant pottery in gay, strong colors. Heavy glass goblets in deep blue, ruby or green would give an added note of interest to the table and the cover should be heavy, natural colored linen or a piece of old blue damask or brocade.

In an interior of this kind it is quite permissible to display choice bits of china and silver on the open shelves of the dresser and in the

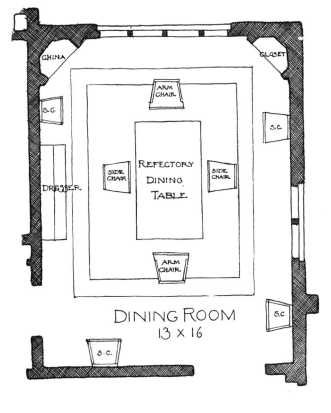

DINING ROOM
13 × 16

corner cupboards. China when used in this manner is extremely decorative, but care should be taken to see that the pieces displayed are really beautiful in line and color and not merely put there to fill up space. Do not overlook the pictorial value of silver and pewter when planning a room of this type. There are lovely reproductions of old English silver now available, simple designs suitable to an interior of this type as well as more elaborate patterns. For the center of the table between meals a reproduction of an old English peony bowl in a graceful fluted design might be used, or a copy of an American compote in gold and white china. Filled with fruit this makes a charming between meal decoration, especially if set on a strip of colorful brocade.

For flat silver a simple William and Mary design would be used.

*The fireplace mirror is a decorative asset and increases the size of the room. The arm chair and hanging bookshelf have been placed convenient to the fire and the casement window*

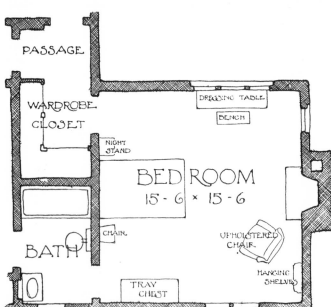

*Furniture in a bedroom should be placed first for convenience for sleeping, second for practicability of light for dressing, and always, naturally, with charm of arrangement in mind*

WHILE a strictly period room is the last thing to be desired, the furnishings of the master's bedroom in this house are in key with the Tudor tendencies of the architecture. The furniture is mostly oak. The warm browns of the wood, brought out by a rich wax finish, and the hand carved moldings and turnings are in keeping with the simple and dignified treatment throughout the house.

On account of the comparatively small size of the room only the necessary pieces are used. A full-sized bed, a dressing table, a bureau, a straight chair, a simple, upholstered chair and a small painted night table are all the furniture required. To this is added a hanging shelf for a few personal books. If a desk is desired, an interesting old oak table might be placed in the space in front of the window at the right of the fireplace.

A restful, practical background of plaster walls painted a rich, deep cream color, glazed with sepia, tones in pleasingly with the dark furniture and colorful draperies and upholstery. The woodwork is painted a darker shade than the walls and the ceiling is light cream. An interesting feature of the room is the floor made of wide boards stained a rich yellow brown and waxed. On account of the color and design in the curtains and upholstery it was thought advisable to use a plain rug here, one made of a wide loom carpeting in a warm tan color—a shade that harmonizes with both walls and furniture.

Chintz is an ideal fabric for the curtains in a room of this character as it has the necessary interest of design and an informal quality that adds to the livable aspect of the interior.

A reproduction of an old chintz was selected for the draperies here —an effective fabric with a background in dull, faded rose color and a decorative pattern of arbors, flowers and birds printed in various shades of tan. Because of the character of the windows only one set of hangings is used. They are lined with sateen and made to pull across the windows at night.

The rose tone is repeated in the material of the bedspread and the covering of the upholstered wing chair which stands at one side of the fireplace. The bedspread is made of dull rose satine, trimmed in tan, with a

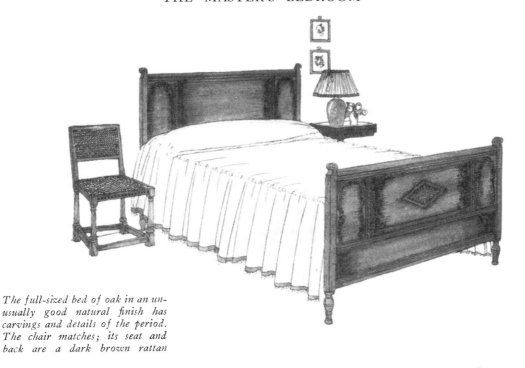

*The full-sized bed of oak in an un-
usually good natural finish has
carvings and details of the period.
The chair matches; its seat and
back are a dark brown rattan*

*Small pedestal table of birch
painted yellow—the top has a rail
and drawer—one of the most convenient small tables on the market*

*36-inch chintz printed in warm
greys and tans on a dull faded
rose. This is an excellent reproduction of an 18th Century
print*

*In this chest for a man's clothes
are trays which conveniently hold
collars, ties and underwear. The
brass handles are in antique finish*

flat bolster pillow to match. The tan appears in the piping at the sides and at the
bottom of the gathered valance which is
cut in scalloped effect.

An effective bit of design is provided by
the material which covers the wing chair
and the cushion on the dressing table bench.
This is a sunfast rep with a rose ground
and a small diamond design in tan and
blue. Or, if preferred, a narrow striped
fabric might be used here in rose and tan
or blue and tan. The only other bit of
pattern appears in the small East Indian
rug in front of the fireplace. This is made
of goat's hair and has a soft dull rose
ground and embroidered figures in brightly

colored wools. The covers of the dressing
table and bureau should be of pink satine
piped in tan. Or a strip of the chintz might
be used, bound with tan satine or taffeta.

Lamps are such important accessories
both from a decorative and utilitarian
standpoint that they should be selected with
the utmost discretion. In this case the lamps
chosen for the dressing table were a pair of
tall, clear glass candlesticks with long
prisms. These are wired for electricity and
fitted with small rose silk shades edged with
narrow French ribbon in shades of tan and
yellow. Their height makes them both
decorative and practical.

The lighting fixtures are reproductions
of old brass candle sconces wired for electricity. These are of two types. Those
flanking the fireplace are three-light affairs
with a narrow urn shaped back, while the
ones on the two side walls have graceful
curved plaques and two candle arms. Other

interesting accessories in this room are a
pair of blue and white Chinese porcelain
jars on the mantelpiece, a graceful clock
with an inlaid walnut case, and a simple
pottery lamp on the small bedside table.
This is rose color with a shade made of
pleated yellow book linen bound at the top
and bottom in pink. This table in contrast
to the rest of the furniture in the room is
painted a clear, warm yellow with stripings in dull rose. Other small objects such
as flower bowls, boxes, etc. should be in rich
yellows and Persian blues. The blue note
is found again in the narrow frame of the
large plate glass mirror over the mantelpiece which is set flush with the wall.

*Cretonne with small all-over pattern background and medallions printed on white, illustrating Aesop's Fables, is in the nursery*

*Reproduction of an old maple butterfly table and shaker chair with removable seat cover of checked gingham. These pieces are practical and at the same time decorative for a nursery*

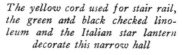

*The tiled bathroom is made interesting by the use of waterproof glazed chintz curtains and a gaily embroidered white Kashmir rug*

*The yellow cord used for stair rail, the green and black checked linoleum and the Italian star lantern decorate this narrow hall*

A PRACTICAL nursery should contain nothing but absolute essentials for the child's comfort and well being. This does not mean that charm has to be sacrificed. Waterproof and sunfast glazed chintzes make the decoration of this type of room a delightfully simple matter on account of their attractive designs and practical wearing qualities. Sunfast and washable rugs also come in designs suitable to a room of this character.

Waterproof and sunfast glazed chintz was selected for the curtains and the cover of the crib. This is plain and gray-blue in color. The window seat cover is of cretonne printed in two tones of blue with a quaint medallion design showing scenes from Aesop's Fables. The floor is hardwood, heavily varnished, and the rug is dark gray with an indistinct all-over design. This type of rug is more practical in a room of this kind than a plain one as it does not show every foot print.

Walls and woodwork painted a soft light gray make a restful and pleasing background for the colorful hangings and furniture. The built-in toy cabinet is given interest by narrow stripings of blue to match the chintz. The window frame is blue and a line of this same color appears in the moldings on the doors. The closet should have built-in drawers and shelves with space allowed for coat hangers to hold the small coats and dresses. The inside of the closet might be painted gray with shelves enameled the same blue as the chintz.

On account of the decided English feeling of the house, reproductions of English or early American furniture were selected. The crib is an adaptation of a sleigh bed and is of wood heavily enameled in blue. The dresser, butterfly table and shaker chair are of maple. The small rocker with its rush seat is a reproduction of an old English farmhouse chair.

Old flower prints are charming in a room of this kind, especially when the frame is painted to harmonize with the scheme of decoration or in some bright, contrasting shade. Here a row of these decorative

*The built-in toy closet is an interesting and archi-
tecturally integral feature as well as the closet with
built-in drawers and shelves*

*Furniture of the simplest form and washable was
selected. The glazed chintz curtains, window seat
and bedspread give the necessary color*

prints is hung above the crib. The narrow frames are painted bright apple green. The shade o nthe lighting fixture is rose colored parchment with lines of decoration at the top and bottom in blue and green.

THE bathroom connecting with this room is of the most approved and up-to-date type. It is tiled up to the cornice with glazed tiles, deep ivory in tone. Color and interest are introduced by the hangings and shower bath curtains of waterproof glazed chintz in rose pink and by the embroidered wool rug on the floor. This has an ivory ground and a decorative flower pattern in many tones. Red glass bottles and linen embroidered in rose add further notes of color.

THE problem of a narrow hall has been most satisfactorily solved. The arch at the foot of the stairway breaks the bleakness of the fundamental wall structure with re-

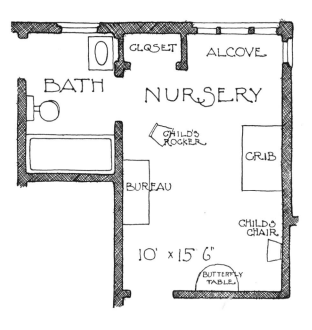

*The plan of the nursery shows that no unnecessary
furniture has been used to make the room difficult
to decorate*

sultant apparent spaciousness and charm. The flooring of black and cream colored tiles, the substitution of a cord for the stair rail, and the star lantern are Italian in feeling, but in many English houses of the Tudor period furniture and accessories of other countries were often used to give interest and variety.

The size of this hall allows for only the merest necessities in the way of furniture. A narrow console and two small straight chairs might be placed in the long wall space on the right side.

Because of the neutral shade of the walls it would be interesting to introduce a bit of color here such as deep green or lacquer red. The console and mirror might be painted rich green with decorations in blue and gold. On the walnut chairs use flat pads covered in blue and yellow striped silk to repeat the yellow note of the stair rail. These colors will enliven the hall.

THE kitchen in this house is made colorful and gay by a scheme of red, yellow and white. The walls are painted pale yellow, the woodwork is enameled a deeper shade of the same color, with stripings of deep rose red. The ceiling is cream toned toward yellow and the floor is hard wood stained very dark brown, with a well-designed rug of linoleum or rubber tile in dark gray.

While no curtains are indicated in the sketch of this kitchen, simple hangings of English print in red and white, trimmed with white rick-rack braid, will add to the livable appearance of the room.

The sink which is conveniently placed between the dresser and the stove is one of the latest patterns, with a swinging faucet and central spout. The trap here is not pictured, but it should be in plain view. It is convenient in all kitchens to have a faucet below the sink from which to fill pails easily.

The furniture is arranged for comfort and convenience. Here you have quite logically the cupboards, the sink, the incinerator chute and the work table. This table can have a wooden top and a rack underneath to hold things. Here, too, can be a metal pull board on which to make pastries. If preferred, a marble top or porcelain top table may be used. The latter type is excellent and

*The kitchen of the Howell & Thomas house has been simply treated and carefully designed for light and convenience. It has an electric stove*

*The plan shows how thoughtfully the circulation has been devised, not only about the kitchen itself, but from there to the dining room and to the hallway*

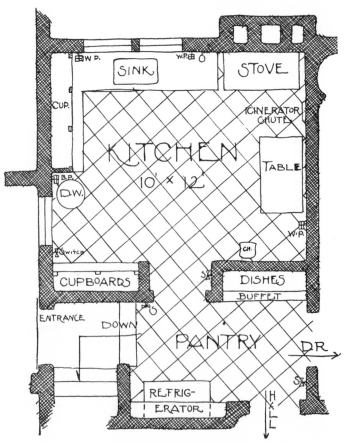

not as expensive as marble would be.

The lighting arrangement here has been carefully thought out. Switches at the right of each entrance save steps and wall outlets allow for present and future appliances. The central fixture is of 100 wattage and will light the kitchen beautifully, while the lights at right and left of the sink will give additional comfort. No reaching is necessary as there is a switch near the left hand sink.

An important feature of the room is the electric range which has the required special wiring. It is of the pattern which cooks firelessly as well. It is equipped with a clock which will, when set, start and cut off the electric current, so that meals may be cooked without supervision.

Another convenience is the dishwasher which is placed near the window with its electric outlet, making this kitchen fairly compact for one of ten by twelve feet.

Aluminum cooking utensils and gay peasant pottery are used here to give additional notes of color. The pantry houses the refrigerator while the "best" dishes are kept in cupboards on either side of the door leading into the kitchen. The shelf space here and in the kitchen does away with the necessity of any show of dishes in a china closet in the dining room.

*At the rear of the plot lies this rectangular space surrounded by a rough stone wall. The near end, lying on a slightly lower level than the ground about it, is the rock garden with its steps and pool. Leading off from it is the little orchard garden*

THE informality of this house has been communicated to its garden. Its picturesque architectural style is reflected in the choice and disposition of the shrubbery and trees, and its irregular plan has been carried over into the arrangement of the grounds.

A curious thing about informality in garden planning is that it is based upon a formal scheme. The informality is only on the surface. Underneath there is orderly arrangement. Otherwise the result would be awkward, disturbing and restless.

The space in the rear of the house has been divided into five parts. First, a more or less oval lawn occupies the center of the scene and is surrounded by a border of shrubbery which forms the background for pockets of perennials. Second, a plot back of the garage which contains four small rectangular beds for vegetables and cut flowers. Third, a heavily planted pathway leading from the covered terrace off the dining room to the rock garden at the rear. Fourth, this rock garden, and

fifth, a tiny orchard garden made possible by some old apple trees, which might be found on any place.

The rock garden and orchard garden are enclosed by a low, roughly built, dry stone wall covered with Roses and Honeysuckle. The level of the rock garden has been made one foot lower than the ground about it so that a few steps could be used. Its floor is a pavement of flagstones.

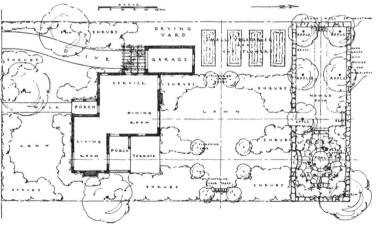

*The grounds are divided into six parts: the service section, from the entrance drive to the vegetable and cut flower beds; the front lawn; the main oval lawn; the long pathway from terrace to rock garden; the rock garden and the orchard garden*

The planting scheme throughout the whole place is held as closely as possible to native plants. The shrubbery planting is composed, among the low-growing types, of such things as:

Ink berry: *Azalea indica*
Indian Currant: *Symphoricarpos vulgaris*
Coral Berry: *Callicarpia purpurea*
Drooping Leucothoe: *L. cathesbei*
Mountain Andromeda: *Pieris floribunda*

Among the shrubs of middle height would be used:

Washington Thorn: *Crataegus cordata*
Red Osier: *Cornus stolonifere*
Golden Willow: *Salix lutea*
Mountain Laurel: *Kalmia latifolia*
Native Rhododendron: *R. catawbiense*
Lilac: *Syringa vulgaris*

Some of the large shrubs and small flowering trees would be:

Flowering Dogwood: *Cornus florida*
Mountain Ash: *Sorbus americana*
Flowering Crabapples: *Malus* (in variety)
Flowering Cherries: *Prunus* (in variety)

*The rambling contours of this house, designed for the
Ideal Smaller Homes Series by Howell & Thomas,
architects, fit easily into the informal scheme of the
grounds. Drawn by Chester B. Price*

# A HOUSE WITH A FRENCH FLAVOR

*Designed for Dignified Suburban*
*Living by Richard H. Dana, Jr.*

IN describing his own house, which is the best way by which it could de described, Mr. Dana says: "Privacy is the keynote of all French houses. The usual gravel forecourt surrounded with a high stone wall would not, of course, be tolerated in the typical American suburb. I have therefore substituted the usual American lawn with low clipped hedge along the sidewalk and property lines.

"I have run the house with its long way parallel to the street, so that the house will screen the private garden on the south from the street on the north. Also, the long side of the house faces the south and garden, and all the rooms face either the street or garden, and not the neighbor's houses or service yards.

"The south terrace makes a warm sheltered place in which to sit and walk in winter, late fall and early spring, as it is protected by the house from the cold north winds. It is well paved so that one can go out there even in muddy weather.

"The exterior walls would be covered with smooth gray stucco, either on wire lath over frame construction or over terra cotta blocks. (An alternative to this would be the use of shiplap—a smooth surfaced weatherboarding.) The windows would be casements, opening in and painted white, most of them going to the floor in the regular way. The blinds would have large fixed slats and be painted white in true French

fashion. The iron railings would be painted black. The hipped roof would be laid with dark slates (or possibly shingles). The chimneys tall and thin, with stucco over brick. The high plain base would be painted a darker gray, thus preventing the splash from the ground showing on the stucco, and also reducing the apparent height of the house. This style, of course, is used a great deal in France. The front door would be of glass in the French mode, which seems to me more informal and inviting than a solid wood door, more commonly used in this country.

"As all streets are now fairly noisy, dusty and public, even in the suburbs, the less important rooms and service are now put on the street front, and the living room and dining room face the garden in the rear where there is sun, quiet and privacy. The ends that come close to the neighbors' houses are used for garage and service respectively.

"The entrance hall is small, but well balanced, with a vista straight ahead through to the garden. There is good wall space for a bench on one side and a table with a mirror over it on the other. The black and white marble floor is practical as well as stylish. The coat closet is conveniently near the front door.

"The stair hall is apart from the entrance hall in order that more privacy may be given the second floor, and also in order that the owner may slip upstairs from the

study or garage without ever being seen.

"The study is well arranged for use, with the desk by a window, and large built-in bookcases. The door to the garage is convenient in rainy weather. The garage is for one car, long enough for the longest made. The extra space at the south end is for the work bench and garden tools.

"The living room has three pairs of French doors opening out onto the terrace, giving the room a splendid view of the garden. The door from the hall is at one end so that two-thirds of the living room around the fireplace enjoys absolute privacy.

"The dining room is small but will give a comfortable seating capacity of eight. The serving pantry is arranged to serve as a buffer between the kitchen odors and the front of the house. It is equipped with a broom closet, in addition to the usual dressers, drainboards and sink.

"The kitchen is small but well arranged, with a dining table under the window. Immediately adjoining is a service hall where the icebox is kept and conveniently iced. Also, the ash cans and garbage cans can be kept here, out of sight from the street, yet very convenient. The inside and outside stairways are combined in one, thereby avoiding the ugly exterior bulkhead, or an areaway that fills with snowdrifts.

"The servant's bedroom is in the wing, conveniently near the kitchen. It is large

*The garden side of this house is splendidly balanced and finely composed. It repeats, with slight variations in the window treatment, the general effect of the entrance façade. Wing walls, shown in the side elevation at the left, separate the long paved terrace from the drying yard at one end and the cold frames at the other*

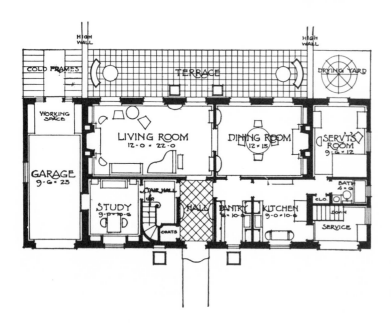

*The first floor plan at the left and the second floor plan below show an arrangement of rooms which, for utilization of space and convenience, could hardly be excelled. The handling of the service section is especially noteworthy, but, for that matter, so is every part of the house, from living room to closets*

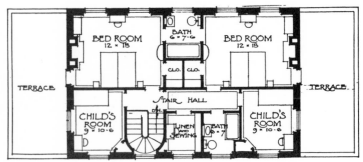

*The simplicity and composure of this rather French house, as shown in the perspective sketch above, are among its most attractive features. It achieves an almost perfect symmetry*

*The plot for this house is perfectly level and faces north. Thus there is no particularly difficult grading or planning problem: simply one of providing an interesting setting*

enough for a man and wife and has splendid cross ventilation with windows south and west. It also has a private bath and closet immediately adjoining.

"The second floor enjoys absolute privacy as there will be no servants sleeping on it or passing through it to rooms above. The hall space is reduced to a minimum so that a very large percentage of the space goes into the four corner bedrooms, each enjoying splendid cross ventilation. Each room has a French door opening onto a terrace or upstairs porch which can be covered entirely or in part with an awning in summer.

"There are two bathrooms, one with a door to the hall for greater flexibility in use. The south bathroom would ordinarily be for the owner's exclusive use.

"When guests are visiting they would have the exclusive use of this south bathroom, and the family would use the bath off the hall.

"None of the bedrooms is large, but they are carefully arranged for the necessary furniture. Each of the double rooms has a fireplace. The small sewing room over the front door is equipped with ample closets for linen, sewing materials, and so on.

The unfinished attic provides excellent air space over the bedrooms and can be reached by a secret disappearing staircase in the hall ceiling.

"Two more points about this house—

"I have entirely eliminated side yards, as these come in too close contact with the neighbors' service doors and consequently have no privacy at all.

"In summer, shade can be obtained from the trees along the rear property lines and also by means of awnings and table umbrellas. Also, in the summer the sun gets round to the north side of the house late in the afternoon, so that the south terrace would be shaded by the house itself after five o'clock, and, consequently, the late afternoon glare avoided.

TERRACE

CONSOLE

*The wall treatment, the windows opening directly on to the flagged terrace overlooking the garden, are all typically French in feeling and in detail*

LIVING ROOM
12' × 22'

→ D.R.

*The plan of the room which shows that the placing of the furniture was influenced by structural requirements and convenience of living*

BOOKS

BOOKS

BERGERE

SOFA    PIANO

TABLE-DESK

CHEST for MUSIC

HALL

THE living room of the small French house combines in true Gallic fashion both simplicity and charm.

The walls, of smooth plaster, are painted a soft grayish green. The wooden mouldings put on to form panels are picked out in pale yellow. The ceiling is a deep cream. The coved cornice is painted the same color as the walls to give more apparent height to the room. The interiors of the built-in bookcases are painted a dark green to give

a note of interest and to display the books to better advantage. The oak parquet floor is stained a dark brown and waxed.

The mantel is a modern reproduction of white marble with yellow veining. The fireplace lining is of black iron or of blackened soapstone. The mirror over the mantelpiece is mounted flush with the wall with narrow wooden mouldings corresponding to the wall treatment.

The rug, a greenish gray wide loom

carpeting, is cut in oval form and bound with self-colored braid.

The curtains are of a heavy yellow satin surfaced sun-fast fabric and are finished with a narrow binding in ashes of roses color. The formal valance repeats this scheme and the tie backs are bands of old needlepoint or cross stitch in dull rich coloring, bound with narrow folds of the yellow and rose.

Two small arm chairs are painted gray

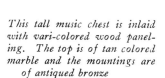

*This tall music chest is inlaid
with vari-colored wood paneling. The top is of tan colored
marble and the mountings are
of antiqued bronze*

*Commode with inlaid vari-
colored wood panels. The
top is of a variegated colored
marble and the mountings
are of antiqued bronze*

and antiqued, and are covered in striped blue and white taffeta and sprigged with small rose colored flower clusters. The bergère is of natural finished wood and is covered with a heavy striped mercerized rep in dull tans and rose. The small side chair is covered in a heavy old rose satin, and is of natural finished wood. The side chair, which is used as a desk chair, is elaborately carved and has a rattan back and seat.

The circular table is of carved wood and has a variegated yellow marble top surrounded with a pierced brass gallery. The tall chest of drawers, used as a music cabinet, and the console, are similar pieces made of inlaid woods with yellow and brown marble tops and bronze mountings in dull antique finish. The table desk is of walnut with a set-in top of a yellow and rose checked fabric, a delightful piece.

*Reproduction of a Sheraton
sofa covered in chintz with
a prune ground. The frame
is mahogany in a dull finish.
The seat is a loose slip cushion*

The sofa, which is a reproduction of a Sheraton model, is covered in dull prune colored chintz with bright floral flower clusters in red, blues and yellows. The frame is mahogany.

Amethyst glass pillar lamps with bronze mountings and shades of tan chiffon are used on the table and desk. Vases of old Chelsea and Chinese pottery in vivid blues and greens are used for flowers. The clock is of dark green marble set off with bronze mountings.

Not a little of the charm of this room is due to the livable manner in which the

furniture is grouped. On either side of the fireplace is a comfortable arm chair. Next to the bergère on the left is a commodious sofa so that three people can converse conveniently or listen to the music. The desk is so placed that the light from the window falls over the left shoulder. This same space on the other side of the door is occupied by a music cabinet in easy reach of the piano which is placed next to the wall with the graceful curved side towards the room. This arrangement leaves the center of the room free, thus creating a sense of space. A rather formal grouping of a table with a chair on either side fills one space between the long windows, the other being occupied by a graceful commode with a variegated marble top and antique bronze mountings. If preferred, a pair of matching chests may be used on either side of the door.

*Reproductions of antique Italian console tables are of walnut in dull finish. Girandoles with dull silver finish mountings have amethyst and crystal pendants. These are equipped for electricity*

THE dining room of our French house echoes the refinement of taste and comfort of living so prevalent among the well-to-do classes in 18th Century Normandy and the Provinces. The walls are painted a lemon yellow with the mouldings, which simulate paneling, lightly glazed in salmon pink. The cornice is glazed to match the walls and the ceiling is a lemon cream. The interiors of the wall cabinets are painted a rich blue. The fireplace is of purple veined marble with steel andirons and firebacks. A parquet floor is stained light brown and waxed. The rug is of tête de nègre wide-loom carpeting bound at each end with self-color braid.

The chairs are copies of an old French chair which shows a strong English influence and a flavor of Normandy. The finish is antique walnut which has been waxed and the rush seats are stained to correspond to the chair coloring. The consoles are Italian, but belong to the same period of Italian furniture as the chairs do of French, so that the fusion of styles is perfect.

This scheme aptly illustrates the possibility of combining pieces of different nationalities in one room. The use of the consoles as serving tables is a noteworthy relief and deviation from the more obvious serving table.

The curtains are in Chinese taste, a note so essential to the decoration of a French room of this period. Their coloring repeats and accents the color scheme of the room. The lighting fixtures are girandoles in dull silver finish with crystal and amethyst pendants. These are wired for electricity.

A charming note in connection with the color scheme of the room is the china—a pottery set copied after an old design. It has a rich cream ground, a shallow scalloped edge, and a rather prim flower design in shades of mauve. With this might be used amethyst glass goblets. In the center of the table is a silver bowl in a fluted design which can be used for fruit or flowers.

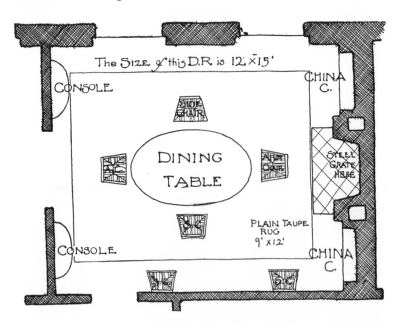

The Size of this D.R is 12'×15'

CONSOLE

CHINA C.

SIDE CHAIR

DINING TABLE

ARM CHAIR

ARM CHAIR

STEEL GRATE HERE

CONSOLE

PLAIN TAUPE RUG 9'×12'

CHINA C.

*Two console tables used as serving tables are placed advantageously near the service door. The oval table detracts from what might otherwise be a monotony of form*

Built-in wall cabinets and French
windows overlooking the garden
give this room an air of interest
and charm effective and unusual

For curtains is used a semi-glazed
36 inch chintz with a background
of sage green on which is a design
in blues, yellows, pinks and tans

Arm chair in an-
tique walnut finish
with rush seat. This
is a reproduction of
an antique French
chair

Toile de Jouy printed in reds on a white ground in
scenes of old Paris. This when varnished makes an
unusual overmantel

Reproduction of an
antique china service
in pottery with a
rich cream ground
printed in shades of
mauve. This is
suggested for the
table service in this
French style of din-
ing room

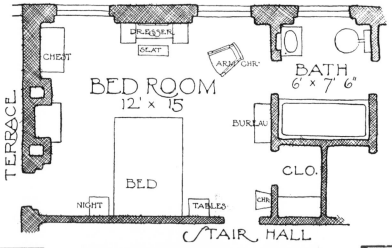

*Consideration of artistic structure and practicability of lighting is evidenced by the placing of bureau and dressing table*

*This copy of an old wall paper has a pattern of green ribbons latticed on a white enameled finish background*

*This plan shows the artistic charm and consideration of personal comfort used by the decorator in planning the floor space*

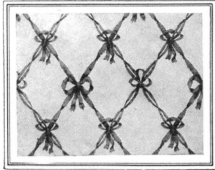

*Opaque green glass bottles and powder box with black glass stoppers and handle. Height of bottles, 5 inches.*

*Papier-mâché box for the man's bureau to hold collars or accessories; hand decorated and lined with marbleized paper*

*A Normandy arm chair of
birch with gaily upholstered
arms, back and seat is conveniently placed by a small
table which holds books and
lamp. The wall pocket is a
warm touch of color*

APPLE green painted furniture with stripings of warm cream, showing Louis XVI influence, was selected for this bedroom in order to strike a note which would be in key with the French feeling of the house's architecture. A full sized bed, dressing table, bureau, bench and side chair are in the green. A Normandy arm chair of birch with blue cretonne printed in a gay floral pattern, a couple of small tables, and a pair of small hanging shelves, complete the furnishings of the room. Girandoles of brass, with clear and amethyst drops, are used for lighting on each bedside table.

The floor of the room is covered entirely with a gray green carpet. The walls are done in a white paper with a green ribbon lattice pattern, and the woodwork is warm cream glazed in green. The ceiling is creamy white. The curtains are of a mercerized rep in wide yellow stripes with narrower ones of rose and blue. A narrow panel of mirror, mounted between strips of wood painted bright blue, may be used for the valance if one desires.

An arm chair, and a tray table with a reading lamp, form a group in a corner of the room. The upholstered peasant type of chair selected gives an appearance of ease and is in effective contrast to the otherwise formal appearance of the room.

The curtains are hung on vivid blue poles with traverse fixtures, which allow them to be easily drawn at night and do away with the necessity of shades.

The use of two mirrors in this room adds to the convenience of living as well as giving vista and a sense of space. Both are framed in narrow moldings painted bright blue to repeat the note of blue in the curtains. The graceful mirror over the

mantel is mounted flush with the wall.

A gay, colorful note in this room is provided by the bedspread which is plain taffeta in primrose yellow. This is trimmed with taffeta cordings in blue and rose—the two main colors in the room. Boxes and toilet bottles on the dressing table and the candlesticks on the mantel are cool green Venetian glass.

The bathroom connecting with this room has a color scheme in harmony. The walls are covered with a fabric treated to give the effect of glazed paper—an extremely practical material as it may be washed. It is a soft, clear green. The curtains are made of yellow waterproof glazed chintz bound in green and the shower bath curtain is green waterproof taffeta. A deep green rug, one small chair painted blue with a cushion covered in pale yellow oil cloth, and green glass toilet bottles complete an unusual and gay little bathroom.

If one prefers, this bedroom might be carried out in a mauve, blue and green color scheme. There is a charming lattice paper in mauve and white which might be used in connection with white woodwork, striped in mauve. In this case the furniture should be painted mauve and decorated with bouquets of old-fashioned garden flowers in soft greens, blues and yellows, or else simply striped in green. Sunfast taffeta in a shade to harmonize with the color of the lattice in the wallpaper would make cool, fresh looking curtains, especially if trimmed with crisp little pleated ruffles put on with a piping of green taffeta. The bedspread might be green taffeta or poplin, scalloped and bound in blue or trimmed with shaded French ribbon in two shades of blue. It would be interesting to paint the floor in this room green and use a deep

violet rug. For a bit of contrasting color cover a small overstuffed chair in peach colored moire corded in mauve. The glass curtains can also be peach color, of either sunfast net, organdie or voile.

In place of a painted dressing table, use a draped dressing table in this room. This should be hung in a chintz with a decided pattern on account of the lack of design in the curtains and rug. A semi-glazed chintz with a peach colored ground and a flower design in soft pinks and mauves would carry out the scheme of the room, especially if trimmed with pleatings of mauve taffeta. Charming Venetian glass toilet bottles are now available in deep purplish color, and the lamps might be a pair of mauve pottery urns with shades of peach taffeta or chiffon trimmed with green ribbon. If more design is needed in this room small Oriental rugs in harmonious colorings might be used on either side of the bed and in front of the dressing table.

Still another interesting scheme for a bedroom of this character would be rose, blue, mauve and yellow. Cover the walls in a toile de Jouy paper, the pattern in deep rose on a white ground, and paint the woodwork white. The curtains can be either of rose taffeta trimmed with knifepleated ruffles put on with a blue piping or else of soft rose gauze hung from an ornamental cornice board and looped back over glass or painted wooden tie-backs. Or, if a very simple bedroom is desired, the curtains might be of white organdie trimmed with three rows of narrow French ribbon in rose, old blue and yellow—or edged with wide fluted ruffles. Drape the dressing table and cover one chair in a blue, rose and yellow chintz.

*A bedroom designed for a young girl has walls covered in a red and white polka dot paper. The curtains and drapery of the dressing table are orchid colored sunfast organdie*

A DAUGHTER'S room should be furnished with the idea of its future possible use as a sitting room, or study. The walls are papered in a white paper, with a red polka dot. The woodwork is painted salmon and glazed lightly with red. The curtains are of orchid organdie with scalloped edge bound in red taffeta. The glass curtains are pink fiber silk net. The ruffles of the dressing table correspond and are mounted over a pink sateen apron to the table.

The dresser, arm chair, chest and seat are reproductions of antiques. The dresser is maple, the chest oak; the Norman French arm chair is covered in a pink and red toile de Jouy print. The bed is a red enameled day bed with plain orchid sunfast cover. The lighting fixtures are copies of old glass lamps wired for electricity, with pleated chintz shades. The carpet is a dark gray with an orchid cast.

Because of the careful arrangement of the furniture a pleasing sense of space is created here. The bed occupies one long wall and the bureau fits nicely into the space between the closet and the door leading into the hall. The graceful draped dressing table is shaped to fit into the corner between the windows and the one overstuffed chair stands directly in front of the other window. This arrangement by leaving the center of the room free adds to the appearance of size.

The study, or library, is furnished with regard to the comfort of the member of the household who will write or read in quiet. The type of desk selected both in construction and size gives ample room for use by two people should they so desire. Comfortable chairs are placed in easy access

to the built-in bookcases with a floor lamp beside them to give correct light for reading. A room like this is a necessity in every household, where one may retire when the hilarity of the living room disturbs one's repose. For this reason all superfluous furniture was discarded and the practical basis of the room was emphasized.

The color scheme of the study is gray woodwork glazed with blue. The interiors of the bookcases are painted vermilion and antiqued. The carpet is a deep blue and the curtains are a yellow silk gauze. The chair covering is blue and yellow striped rep trimmed with a narrow vermilion braid.

The coloring of the walls and woodwork has been kept neutral both for restfulness and to increase the sense of size. To avoid coldness and monotony, color has been introduced in the bookshelves and in the gauze silk curtains.

A splendid wall composition has been given the window side of the room where the casement is flanked by inset bookcases which fit perfectly the side spaces. Above the shelves are panels which might be filled in with old prints or paintings.

In a room of this character may be hung old maps, colored prints, or etchings. They will give interest and detract from the severity of plain walls.

In fact, one's pet fad, be it autographs, sport prints or old paintings, may be indulged in with freedom as far as one's purse strings will tolerate and wall space allows.

Considering its size, the small hall in this house has been given unusual distinction. The walls are painted antique cream and glazed with red. A line of red in the mold-

ings accentuates this color note which appears again in the frame of the mirror over the wrought iron console.

An interesting feature of this hall is the use of painted panels at various intervals. These successfully break up the wall spaces and bring a bit of design into the room. The coloring of these panels is mostly green, with here and there a note of red and vivid blue. Flowered wallpaper or a paper with a Chinoiserie design would give much the same effect.

Only the essential furniture is used here. On one side is a wrought iron console with a decorative pedestal made of arrows. The top is marbleized wood in cream and black. Over this hangs a simple mirror with a painted red frame and on the opposite wall is a long narrow bench painted red with a cushion in red and cream striped rep. The floor is covered in black and cream linoleum in a block pattern.

Distinctive lighting fixtures have been used in both the small study and hall. On the wall opposite the console in the hall is a pair of Directoire candle brackets in dull gilt finish, touched here and there with black. These are in the form of arrows, to repeat the arrow motif of the iron console. The lighting equipment in the study consists of a floor lamp, a pair of lamps on the desk and two side brackets. The slender floor lamp is metal with a graceful urn shaped top. It is painted dull blue striped in red and has a tan parchment shade with a painted design in both these colors. The lamps on the desk are reproductions of old French silver lamps. They have adjustable arms and small square tin shades painted red and decorated with a laurel leaf design in gold.

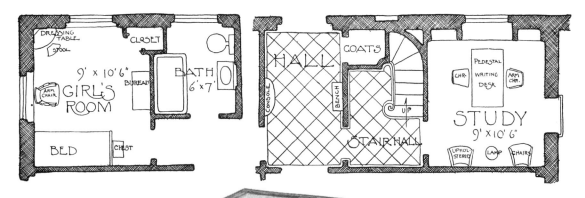

The placing of the furniture against the wall leaves enough floor space to give the room an appearance of considerable size

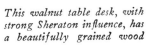

In planning the arrangement of the study due regard has been given to the charm as well as the convenience of the scheme

This antique Jacobean carved oak chest reproduction has richly paneled top and sides

This French bergère reproduction has a frame in walnut finish and loose cushion seat

This walnut table desk, with strong Sheraton influence, has a beautifully grained wood

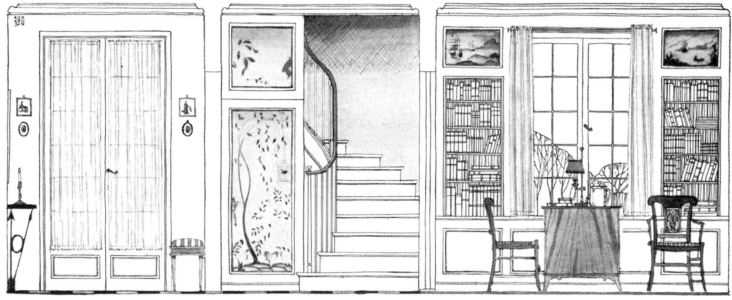

The desk is placed to take every advantage of the light, and also for the convenience of two people

The built-in bookcases are open. Above them, old marine prints are mounted flush to the wall

*The kitchen in Mr. Dana's French home is not only extremely workable, but pleasantly livable as well; gay in color and good in design*

I N THIS kitchen the color scheme can be gray, blue and white or rose and white.

On the floor you can have rubber tile or linoleum with repeating dark gray and white squares. Preferably a small square. Of course, this must be well laid with the curved join to the wall, a sanitary cove.

The wall is painted gray or rose, as the case may be, with blue or gray rail. This rail is put here to save the wall wounds, due to too ardent intimacies between furniture, hands and walls.

The ceiling is pale gray, a tone just off the white, without the glare and very satisfactory.

The curtains are of blue check either of oil cloth or gingham, and give the kitchen a livableness that is delightful.

In front of the window is a small table which folds down so as to be out of the way. This is painted in light blue to tone

with the curtains and blue wood of the base board and the rail. The chairs too, can be painted blue, an easy thing to do with any inexpensive chair. Or they may be white striped in blue.

The laundries of these houses, except on one set of drawings, are not pictured, as they reside in the cellar. However, this would show but the placing of the two tubs and the electric outlets—to which would be attached the electric ironer, electric washer and electric iron. Houses as amply supplied with electric outlets as these will always preserve a great elasticity in the arrangement and rearrangement of equipments. The chief reason why laundries and kitchens today are so inconvenient is that the outlets and lighting fixtures are badly placed, making the equipment bend to the electric malfeasance instead of the electric outlets bending to the proper placing of the equipment. Note, too, the electric light

switches at the right of each door in all of these kitchen and pantry plans.

If the purse is able to stretch far enough the incinerator for waste and refuse is ideal. Especially in remote regions where there is no system for garbage disposal. Failing this, the white enamel can or garbage container, the lid of which is lifted by pressing a pedal with the foot, is an excellent substitute for the garbage chute. It is often wise, where there is a stationary garbage incinerator in the kitchen, or chute to the cellar incinerator, to have an hygienic can of this type in the pantry.

From a purely pictorial standpoint this small kitchen is unusually effective. In addition to the colorful background and gay checked curtains is the interest of a tiled wall behind the sink and work tables. The tiles are white with a prim flower design in colors, adding vastly to the decorative appearance of the room.

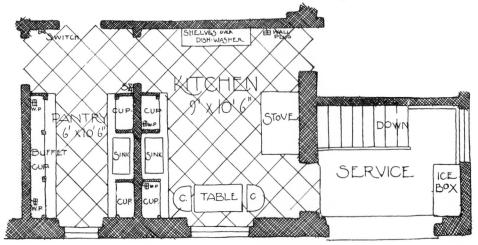

*Mere space in a kitchen is less important than completeness, compactness and convenience. Here the unit comprising pantry, kitchen and service entry has been planned with unusual ingenuity*

THE grounds whose arrangement and planning are described here are those for the house designed by Richard H. Dana, jr., architect. The house, being rather French in feeling, with a stuccoed exterior and a definitely formal appearance, gives an opportunity to do a garden in the French manner, something rarely attempted in this country except in imitations of the grand and florid fashion of France's most pretentious period.

In this case simplicity has been the quality sought—simplicity, directness, and discretion in the use of plants. All these are characteristic traits of the smaller and unaffected French gardens, both old and modern. In one sense of the word there is no definite garden although there is a small garden plot on either side of the broad *tapis vert* that stretches from the terrace to the rear property line. These small garden plots, however, are only incidentally decorative. One is devoted to neat-growing vegetables and the other to flowers for cutting. They are not meant to make any particular display, and are merely pleasant things to see in passing.

The site is level and faces north: almost ideal conditions from the standpoint of ease and convenience in planning and executing work on the grounds. Scarcely any

*Against the rear garden wall, arched at this point and pierced by a circular opening, stands this graceful, cross-arched pavilion of lattice. It is on the axis of the tapis vert and is flanked by two clipped privets*

*At the end of each side path, bordered by dwarf fruits, stands an urn on a stone shaft, as an architectural accent to close the vista*

*The planting diagram below shows with what simplicity the whole place has been planned. The numbers refer to plants named in text*

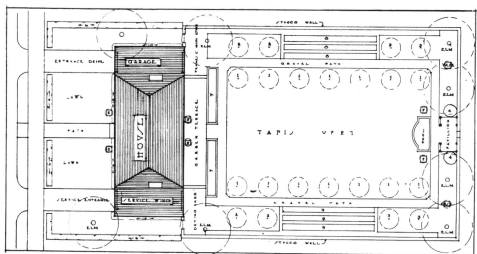

grading is necessary, and the exposure for both garden and house is perfect. These are important factors in the design, and their influence becomes quite obvious as the development of the plan is followed.

The principal part of the garden is the great open panel of turf, flanked by rows of dwarf apples. The eye is carried across its smooth green surface to a cross-arched pavilion, done in lattice, whose graceful, delicate lines are reflected in a brimming pool. A gravel path, with well kept edges, surrounds this *tapis vert* and forms the connecting link between terrace and pavilion, and provides, as well, access to the small garden plots and the service spaces on either side of the house. At the end of each side path, looking from the house end of the garden, stands a vase on a shaft—a crisp architectural note to close the vista.

The whole garden space—in fact, all the property from the south façade of the house to the rear boundary line, is enclosed within a six-foot wall, stuccoed to match the house. The protection this affords and the splendid framework it provides for the garden are things which the French appreciate intensely. A garden there, in town or country, would no more be built without a surrounding wall than a house would be made without rooms.

With the exception of such things as grape vines against the garden walls and flowering vines on the little pavilion all the planting on the place is indicated by the numbered spaces on the plan. Item Number 1, for instance, should be some suitable variety of Dwarf Apple—a kind of tree to stand from ten to fourteen feet high. Number 2 marks the location of Dwarf Pears of a similar size, and Number 3 Peaches.

If there is no particular desire for the Pears and Peaches, all the trees along the paths might be Apples. The latter, while they may have rivals in the spring when Cherries are in bloom, stand alone in excellence. Hardly any other kind of tree achieves such rich delightful beauty. In blossom its loveliness cannot be surpassed, and at every other season its gnarled and nicely balanced form gives it a unique charm. Placed along either side of a path, as has been done here, and then this double line duplicated across a flat sweep of greensward, is to create an effect with these delightful trees which can only become more and more beautiful as time goes on.

The two Number 4's, on either side of the pavilion, are clipped Privets as shown in the sketch at the top of page 61. Two substitutes in this place for Privet, if they can be afforded, are Box or Yew. The former should be well selected specimens of *Buxus suffruticosa,* the true Dwarf Box, and the latter should be *Taxus cuspidata.* Box should be given a sheltered location north of New York, while the *Taxus* is generally able to withstand severe climates, after it has once become established, without particular protection.

Number 5's are Bay Trees or Oleanders set out in tubs in Spring and taken in when frost arrives. Number 6 represents a hedge of Barberry which surrounds the front section of the property where it is pierced by the garage and service entrances and the entrance path. Number 7 marks the two long beds of annuals fronting the terrace. The narrow panels marked 8 constitute the small vegetable plot, while Number 9 marks the cutting garden opposite. The foundation planting before the house has been made appropriately effective by giving it simplicity almost to the point of severity. It consists altogether of Evergreen Bittersweet (*Euonymous radicans vegetus*), which provides a dark green border along the base of the building at every season. If the severity of the front lawn fails to fit the taste of the owner, it may be relieved by planting six Dogwoods across the front, just inside the hedge and on either side of each path and driveway.

The terrace carries across the garden face of the house between two wing walls

which separate it from the gardener's working space at one side and the drying yard at the other. It is paved in tiles and is set with groups of iron garden furniture in graceful and delicate lines.

The existing growth on the site consists of several large Elms, four of which are disposed along the rear property line and the rest clustered about the house. The subsequent planting has been planned with great economy in the choice and number of plants used. The result is a place whose upkeep can never become a burden. Everything has been done for convenience and

for facilitating the gardening operation.

Scarcely enough can be said for this scheme of gardening—especially on a place of this kind in the suburbs, where so often there seems to be little time for actual garden work on the part of the owner, and where an all-time gardener would mean too great an expense. Much of the loveliness of such a garden as this depends upon its trimness. The stretch of lawn in the central panel must be well cut and in good condition. If it were more irregular in shape its cutting and care would require considerably more effort and pains, but as

it has been planned here it is a matter of plain, straightaway mowing. The size of the vegetable and cutting gardens is neither too large to demand any great amount of time in cultivation, nor too small to provide all the fresh vegetables and flowers necessary. A full day's work once a week during spring, summer and fall should be plenty to keep the place in perfect order. Once a year the trees should be pruned and sprayed and minor repairs made to the walks.

It is almost essential that the scheme of this garden be carried out on a plot of ground which is quite level. It would

*This drawing of the whole place, done by Chester B. Price, shows how carefully have been kept the essential qualities of unaffected French gardens—simplicity, restraint, and directness, resulting in remarkably low upkeep and ease of operation*

hardly do for an appreciable slope to exist without robbing the design of its most effective quality. If the site should happen to be on a grade, that part of it from the garden side of the house to the rear of the property should be made level. If that is impossible, the scheme as shown here should either be abandoned or radically

changed to suit the different conditions. There can be no compromise between a design of this kind and a piece of uneven topography. If the scheme does not fit the ground, the ground must be made to fit the scheme, or another scheme devised.

The enclosure here is quite as important as the wood of the garden. The sort of wall shown is more in keeping with the design of the garden than any other type of surrounding screen, but if something else were to be necessary—a hedge or lattice, then the alternative should be kept to a very trim and formal shape.

# HOUSE & GARDEN'S
# INFORMATION
# SERVICE

*To Those Who Build,*

*Decorate and Garden*

HOUSE & GARDEN maintains an Information Service which offers prompt and authoritative solutions of problems on building and architecture, furnishing and decoration, and the making and maintenance of gardens. These problems are studied and their questions answered by authorities on each subject—an architect for the building questions, a trained decorator for furnishing and decoration and an experienced landscape architect for the garden questions.

The dispatch and helpfulness with which these questions are answered depends mainly upon the clearness with which the questions are asked. Photographs and rough plans of the house should accompany the building questions, a clear description of the rooms the decorating problems, and a scaled drawing of the garden plot for the landscape question. We do not sell plans of either houses or gardens.

HOUSE & GARDEN renders this service gratis. Questions should be sent, accompanied by a stamped addressed envelope, to HOUSE & GARDEN's Information Service, 19 West 44th Street, New York City

# THE ELEMENTS OF
# HOUSE CONSTRUCTION

*The Building Process From*
*Foundation to Roof*
*Graphically Explained*

Gillies

## GABLES GALORE

*Such an interesting and picturesque arrangement
of roof lines as this could scarcely fail to cover
an equally interesting interior; and that is the case
here in the house of John E. Sheridan at Port
Washington, N. Y.   Wesley Bessell, architect*

# THE PICTURE AS A WHOLE

*Architects, Decorators and Landscape Architects Help*

*Visualize the House that the Owner Makes a Home*

FOR the average man the building of a house is an adventure, a voyage over seas that are not completely charted, an expedition into worlds with only a few highways and many deceiving bypaths. He approaches the venture either recklessly or cautiously.

When an amateur is considering an expedition into the Artics, he usually seeks the advice and suggestions of such hardy explorers as Capt. Bob Bartlett or Roald Amundsen; when he thinks of venturing on the task of building a house he seeks the advice of such pilots as architects, decorators and landscape architects. And he does this not only because the architect knows how a house is built, or a decorator how rooms are furnished or a landscapist how a garden is laid out, but because each of these professions has been trained to see many more things and see further and deeper than the untrained amateur eye.

The amateur may think in terms of pleasant windows or picturesque doorways, but the architect thinks of a mysterious thing called mass. You may have all the picturesque doorways and windows in the world, but if the mass of your house is wrong, the house will be wrong. In the same way the decorator speaks professionally of color values and scale, which are subtle matters that the amateur may not easily grasp. Equally difficult is it to understand why the landscape architect insists so much on design when what you want is a pretty garden with plenty of flowers.

To the professionally trained mind these are fundamental affairs; upon them depends the success of a house. Because they are grounded in these fundamentals, the vision of the professional mind is more comprehensive than the conglomerate ideas of the lay mind.

EACH of us, when we come to build that house, has a notion of the sort of house we want, but in nine cases out of ten we do not realize either what that sort of house requires or what it can become when it is fully developed. We fail to see the picture as a whole.

Of what does the whole picture consist?

It consists of the relation of the house to its site, to its exposure, to its environments of nature and neighbors. It consists of mass, of roof lines and windows and doors, of room leading to room, of closets and stairs. It consists of the strength and color and texture of building materials and the effect they have when knitted together into a façade. It consists of light and shade, of scale and balance of openings, of delicacy or power or picturesqueness or traditional line. It consists of good engineering, adequate lighting, sanitary plumbing. These are a few of the things that contribute to the whole picture of a house.

Equally complicated and numerous are the things that go to furnishing rooms in which you delight and gardens that give you touch with immortality and make life worth living.

To command all this knowledge a man would have to be a paragon, he would have to study the years of many men's lives.

If, then, he would have his house and his rooms and his garden a success, let him seek the services of those who have devoted their lives to these especial problems.

But, you protest, shall I surrender myself completely to this trio of—well, luxurious professionals?

This is the last thing an architect or a decorator or a landscapist wants; in fact, the houses and gardens where they are given *carte blanche* are rarely successful. For these professions may furnish knowledge and understanding and a vision of the thing you want, but they cannot do it alone. The owner and the owner's desires and dreams, his habits and his ambitions, his manner of living and the manner in which his family lives—these are the vitalizing elements necessary to bring the work of the architect, the decorator and the landscapist to the attainment of their plans.

Like a new motor that has to be run several hundred miles before it is really in good condition, so a new house must be lived in for some time until it begins to bear the aspects of a home. Gradually, as the days pass, the newness wears off, the garden grows, the chairs are shifted about to afford desirable comfort and convenience; gradually the owners become a part of the house and the house a part of them. And that is the thing that no architect or decorator or landscape architect can give; you must live in your house, must be content to be there, must be happier there than anywhere else, if you wish to see the picture as a whole.

BUT there are two matters which the most untrained layman can study and control to his heart's delight and the benefit of his mind—the methods of building and the materials used. On the following pages those methods are outlined. The building materials is another story.

In the course of building a house there comes a time when one's extravagances begin to loom ominously. The first bill for building materials reads like an accusation. You start with good intentions to use only the best materials—and then you see what the best materials cost. That, sirs, is a time when the heart needs courage. It is a time to keep the head level. To weaken one's good intent at that point is fatal.

In the long run the best materials cost only a little more than the cheapest. That insulation on walls and roof, that better kind of prepared shingle, that better brick, that better flooring, that better paint—these things cost more because they are intrinsically worth more than shoddy materials. Combined, they make a better appearing house. They make a house that is easier to live in and they are a source of pride.

*This type of house with long horizontal lines is suitable for a moorland site, where the lines of the landscape are horizontal, and tall trees are not a factor*

# RELATING A HOUSE TO ITS SITE

*Where there is a heavily wooded background only the front of the house is a visible factor in its setting, consequently any type of house with a picturesque or dignified front façade would be suitable*

*An old village site where venerable elms and weathered gray stone walls direct the builder's choice to a house that will be true to the type found in the locality. Sketches by Frank J. Forster, architect*

*(Below) A thickly wooded hilltop site suggests a type of house that will rise above the trees and whose roof lines will carry on the steep profile of the hill*

*On a hillside site bare of trees the house should utilize both its profile and its mass to counteract the slope and still appear stable itself, as shown below*

*Happy relationships of house and site do not come ready-made. They are the result of someone's careful thought and study—of the owner's or the architect's, or of both in an intelligent meeting of minds. This new house with an old profile is designed to take its place agreeably in the orchard of an abandoned farm site*

# HOW TO READ HOUSE PLANS

*Some Suggestions for Solving the Mysteries of Scale Drawings*

*for Those Who Would Attempt to Make or Read Them*

OFTEN all has gone happily enough on the projected house until the first look at the plans, on each of which appears the legend, modestly lettered in one corner, "¼ Inch One Foot", or "¼″ 1′0″", the latter employing the architect's and builder's symbol of (′) instead of the word "foot", or "feet", and (″) in place of the word "inches".

"What does he mean, 'a quarter of an inch equals a foot'? A quarter of a dollar doesn't equal a dollar."

The whole thing is simplified if you read it "represents" instead of "equals."

On the architect's drawings, that is on the scale drawings of plans and elevations, every quarter of an inch represents a foot on the actual house. The adoption of a quarter of an inch to represent a foot, instead of a half an inch, is simply a standardized form of procedure, a convention, used by all architects because its customary use makes it easier for contractors and the men on the job to "read" the plans.

This "quarter of an inch" which represents a foot is the "scale" at which the drawing is made. Other scales are used for other drawings, but the working plans from which the blue prints are made, are always "¼ inch scale drawings."

What happens if you try to make a set of plans, even roughly, without making them "to scale"? Everything is guess work. The hallway which you mean to be 4′ wide is nearer 6′, compared with some other guessed-at dimension, and a room which you mean to make 14′ x 20′ may be nearer 10′ x 18′. Nothing will work out on such a guess-work plan even closely enough to determine the possibilities not to speak of the actualities of the proposed house. The amateur planner, too, has the utmost difficulty in getting the upper floor plans to correspond with the first floor plan.

It is a simple enough matter to make a set of preliminary plans to scale, and simpler still to read scale plans. But no one should make the mistake of thinking that "scale" is all that's needed on a set of actual working drawings from which a house can be built. Scale will make the difference between a set of ideal plans for a house which are absurd and impractical and a set of plans which can be used as a reasonable point of departure for a set of working plans.

The architect's quarter-inch scale plans carry all the dimension figures as well,

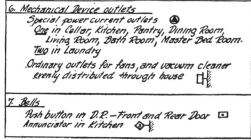

*The working drawings contain symbols for electric outlets, as shown in this fragment. From "The Construction of the Small House" by H. V. Walsh*

notes, reference to specifications and detail drawings and the correct indication for fireplaces, flues, stairways, heating, plumbing and electric outlets, with much other essential detail impossible for the amateur planner to incorporate in his rough layouts.

In "reading" quarter-inch scale plans with an ordinary foot rule, the procedure is as simple as possible. If a room measures 2½′ wide, that is ten quarter inches, and as a quarter inch represents a foot, the room is 10′ wide. Without the definiteness of using a uniform scale throughout a set of plans, nothing in the planning of the house could be definite, and it would be impossible for a builder to construct the house.

For details of fireplaces and unusually complicated stairways a still larger scale is often used, in which an inch and a half is used to represent a foot. Scale drawings are very seldom made larger than this, and the next scale used is actual size, which is not a scale at all. These drawings are usually marked "F.S.D.," meaning "full size detail", and are made to show the profile of moldings and the construction of elaborate cabinet work.

On the quarter-inch scale drawings these notes often appear, "See ¾ scale detail", or "See F.S.D.", thus informing the builders that carefully detailed drawings of these portions have been, or are being made. No architect makes scale or full size details until the final approval of the quarter-inch scale drawings of the whole house.

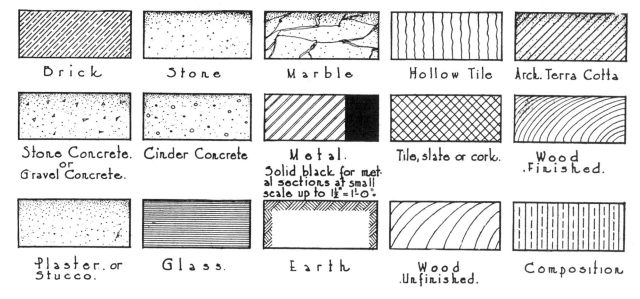

*Every conceivable form of building material has its symbolic marking on a plan. The above are only a few of the symbols used. Read your plans and specifications before the house is started, and you will grasp its construction. From "Good Practice in Construction" by P. K. Knobloch*

Broken corners and ir-
regular lines lend inter-
est and help to reveal
the real nature of the
slates

Closed and rounded
valleys give continuity
to roof surfaces which
are broken by dormers
and gables

*If the slates are heavy, or throw strong shadows throughout a great
expanse of roof, the house walls below should appear equal to sus-
taining comfortaby the roof load above. Cross & Cross, architects*

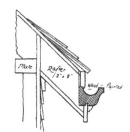

Wooden Gutter worked
out of solid piece

Section showing Tile Roof

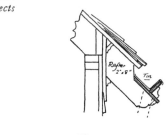

Tin-lined Gutter

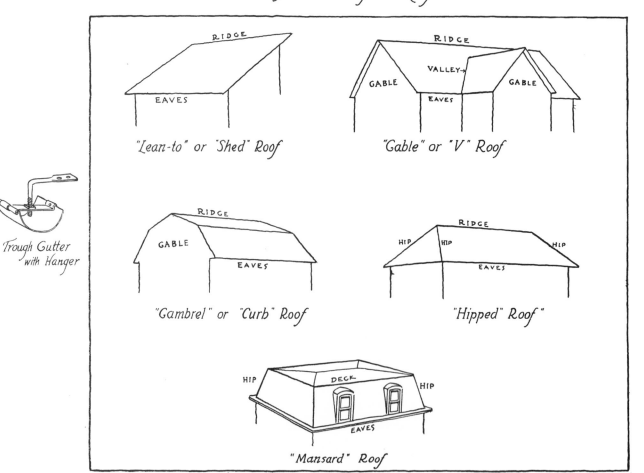

Trough Gutter
with Hanger

"Lean-to" or "Shed" Roof

"Gable" or "V" Roof

"Gambrel" or "Curb" Roof

"Hipped" Roof"

"Mansard" Roof

Ornamental Cap
on Metal "leader"

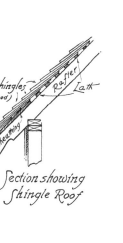

*Section showing
Shingle Roof*

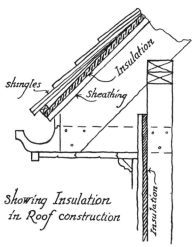

*Showing Insulation
in Roof construction*

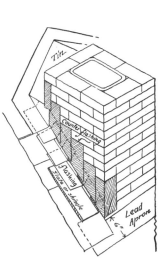

*Chimney Flashing*

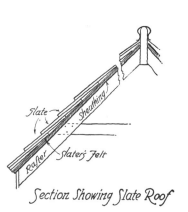

*Section Showing Slate Roof*

*The most important factor in the successful design of this house by H. T. Lindeberg is the great expanse of roof above the fieldstone walls*

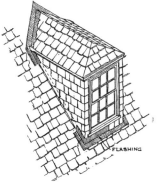

FLASHING FOR DORMER
ON SHINGLE ROOF

*On these two pages are shown the essentials of roof construction and some of the materials used; other suggestions will be found on page 76*

# ROOFS IN CONSTRUCTION
# AND ARCHITECTURAL DESIGN

*Sand struck, soft mud bricks are in this house laid in English bond, with raked joints. The brick work scales beautifully with the glass sizes and with the roof slates. Harrie T. Linde-berg, architect*

# USING   BRICK
### *to*
# ADVANTAGE

*A Colonial brick laid in Flemish bond, with alter-nating headers and stretch-ers in each course, and with concave tooled joints*

*This brick, a "Harvard" type, is laid up in English bond—with alternating header and stretcher cours-es, making variation*

*(Left) Two hand molded, soft mud, sand struck bricks from Virginia with their unusual variation in shape, size and color. (Above, left) The upper of the two is a stiff mud, shale brick; the lower a sand struck, soft mud "Balti-more." (Above, right) The upper is a "Star Colonial Clinker," the lower a "Harvard." (Right) The upper is a wire cut, the lower a raked, stiff mud, shale brick*

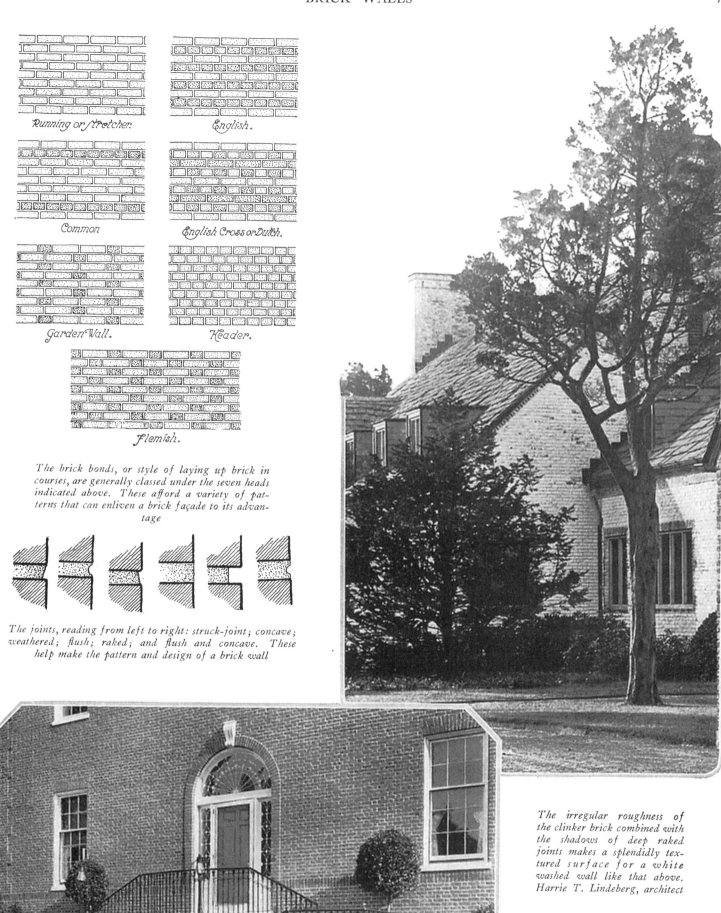

Running or Stretcher.

English.

Common

English Cross or Dutch.

Garden Wall.

Header.

Flemish.

The brick bonds, or style of laying up brick in courses, are generally classed under the seven heads indicated above. These afford a variety of patterns that can enliven a brick façade to its advantage

The joints, reading from left to right: struck-joint; concave; weathered; flush; raked; and flush and concave. These help make the pattern and design of a brick wall

The irregular roughness of the clinker brick combined with the shadows of deep raked joints makes a splendidly textured surface for a white washed wall like that above. Harrie T. Lindeberg, architect

What could harmonize more perfectly with the delicate late Georgian detail of door-way, rail and steps of the Burden house than this closely laid white jointed brick work? Delano and Aldrich, architects

*In the house of Vernon Radcliff, Pelham, N. Y., S. F. Hunt, architect, stone, **timber** and **stucco** are joined*

*To relieve the expanse of stucco on the wall to the right, the door way is surrounded by brick quoins and a stone lintel. E. L. Palmer, architect*

## THE TEXTURE OF

## WALLS

*Stone cropping out through stucco makes an interesting wall treatment especially in rugged type of houses as at the left. C. J. Sweeterman, architect*

*With adz-hewn timbers and rough-textured brick masonry, leaded casements and wrought iron are splendidly appropriate. J. W. Day, Douglaston, N. Y., owner; Frank Forster was the architect*

*Stained shingles with white trim is a combination that can be recommended for country houses. Patterson-King, architects*

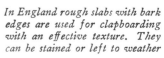

*In England rough slabs with bark edges are used for clapboarding with an effective texture. They can be stained or left to weather*

*Clapboards of irregular sizes are used on this American house in much the same manner as rough slabs in England. Wesley Bessell was the architect*

*Hand-split shingles painted white make the ideal walls for a Colonial type of country house. They are used here with a decorative molding. Peabody, Wilson & Brown, architects*

*Wide flat boards laid up with deep raked joints is the style used on this California bungalow of which Donald P. McMurray was architect*

# WALLS OF
# WOOD

This roof is laid with copper shingles, in a range of colors which are part of the copper itself

Stained shingles laid in irregular wavy courses produce a roof of interestingly "antique" appearance

A roof of vigorously rugged character and texture is effected here by good use of tapered asbestos shingles

# SHINGLES IN MODERN

# VARIETY

This softening of sharp gables and eaves, by the thatch effect in laying, is achieved with wood shingles

Laying asbestos shingles over an old roof, the roofer uses beveled strips of pine to make an even surface

Vari-colored asbestos shingles create a roof with an interesting mixture of tones in harmonious natural shades

Here asbestos shingles, laid to form apparently hexagonal units, are being placed directly over an old wood shingle roof

The thatch effect has now been achieved with copper shingles. The color here is the natural oxidized green of the copper

# HINTS FOR BUILDERS AND BUYERS

*Some Points to Watch in the*

*Building of a New House*

IN EITHER buying or building a house several points should be carefully investigated:

1. See that the bearing plates on the main foundation walls are properly bedded in cement mortar before any joists and studding are put on. Do not allow the plates to be laid directly on the masonry work to be pointed up later. A full bed of mortar should be spread on top of the foundation and the plates then tamped into it before the cement has set. In this way all the unevenness of the wall is taken up and wind and cold cannot possibly get through.

2. See that there is no connection between the chimney and any part of the frame work. The chimney should be entirely independent of any woodwork, especially if the house is built on soil which is likely to settle.

3. Be sure that good water-proof paper is put behind all four sides of the window frames before they are nailed into the walls. At the bottom of the frame, under the sill, the paper should be nailed into the sill and then run out and wedged into the groove in which the siding fits, the surplus being cut off flush with the siding. This point, if not made tight, is where most of the wind comes in around a framed window.

4. How many homes have you been in where the floor looks as though it were dropping down, especially on an inside wall over a furnace, near a heat pipe or register? This defect is generally caused by the shrinking of the floor joists, due in most cases to severe heat from furnace or pipes, and can quite easily be overcome. The usual hurry-up construction is to nail the baseboard to the studding, then to nail the carpet strip to the baseboard, so that the painter may finish the entire two members as one. This looks well for a time, but as the joists shrink the opening between the floor and the carpet strip appears. The following procedure should be observed to overcome the difficulty: After the base has been nailed to the wall, the painter should finish this single member entirely to the floor-line. The carpet strip should then be painted or stained, as the case may be, before it is nailed into place. When the floors have been scraped and finished the carpet strip is nailed—not to the baseboard, but by slanting the nail into the floor. The nail holes in the carpet strip are then puttied up and this member given a final coat of enamel or varnish according to the requirements. The joists may now shrink and the floor strip go down the full height of the carpet strip, but there will still be a tight intersection between base members and also between carpet strip and the floor.

5. To avoid the shrinking and cracking of floors, you cannot take too much care in the laying of the flooring. Circulars issued by large flooring manufacturers may be sent for and studied and instructions followed, such as, "flooring must be delivered when thoroughly dry and must be kept dry; all plastering must be dry and the house heated, etc." This should apply to every home built, but in a great many houses, especially in the less expensive ones, it is almost impossible to fulfill all these requirements. In a great many houses the sub-floors are omitted and the finish floors are put down before plastering is done; this is especially true of the second floors. Sub-floors, including a good grade of paper, should be used, at least on the first floor. The cost is only about five cents a square foot. In addition to this,—and it becomes a necessity if sub-floors are not used down stairs,—nail to the bottom of the floor joist some kind of fire-proof wall-board or plaster-board over an area of at least ten feet square directly over the furnace. This will deflect the intense heat which is bound to be found directly over the furnace and heat pipes, and relieves the flooring and floor joists of the extreme heat.

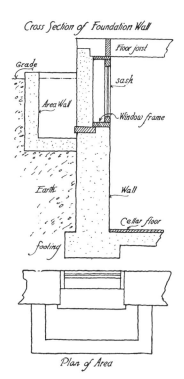

*Cross Section of Foundation Wall*

*Plan of Area*

*The story of the building of a foundation wall is graphically explained in this diagram*

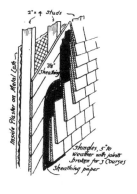

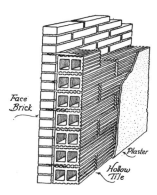

*Section of 13 inch Wall Showing Method of backing face brick with hollow tile*

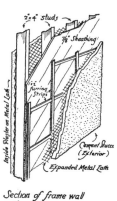

*Section of frame wall Showing method of applying Cement Stucco*

Paint and stain can work miracles in the appearance of a floor. The oiled and waxed floor is desirable in many types of rooms. Paint is advisable for an old floor, especially in a country house, where a plain color or a Colonial spatter may be used

Parquet flooring comes in a vast variety of designs and in a number of beautiful woods

# THE CONSTRUCTION

# AND

# DESIGN OF FLOORS

Flooring of the parquet type is made up into patterns fitted together and ready to lay

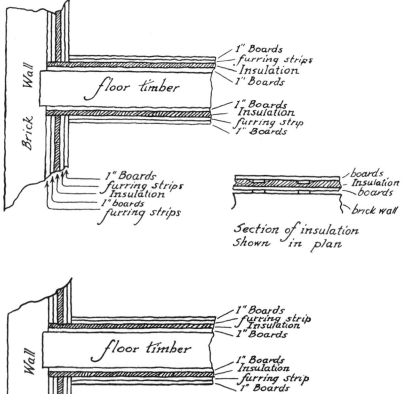

Insulation is the logical way of making a floor draft and sound proof. The material is placed between the sub-floor and the top

The furring strips over the insulating material are shown below. Building paper is laid between the floors when no insulation is used

Section of insulation shown in plan

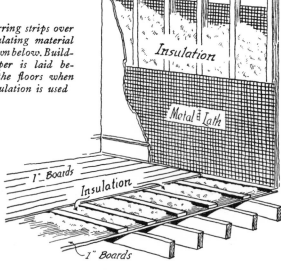

Method of Construction for the use of Insulation in Walls and Floors

Porches, terraces and sunrooms may have tiled floors. A great variety of colors and designs are available. Andrew J. Thomas was the architect of this tiled sunroom

An unusual flooring consists of Oak strips, 1⅜ inches wide, divided by a quarter-inch strip of Maple soaked in lamp black

One of the simplest parquet designs is made of squares of strips of contrasting Oak. It is suitable for an English room

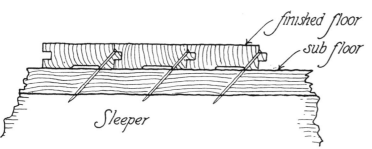

Double (wooden) floor - Section showing concealed nailing

Sub-flooring is laid diagonally. It is usually three-sixteenths of an inch thick and about three inches wide. On this the finished floor is fastened by blind nailing

Cork and composition and linoleum tile floors are coming into wider use, not only in the service alone, but in the living quarters of the house

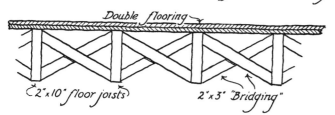

Cross-Section showing method of bridging between floor joists to prevent them from twisting and buckling sidewise

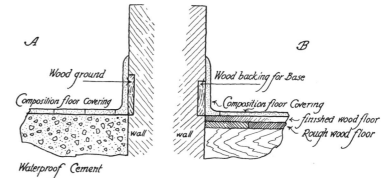

Composition floor covering
A - Laid on Concrete Base    B - Laid on Wood Base

# VARIOUS USES FOR MOLDINGS INDOORS AND OUT

*Elegance and interest are given the door of this latticed garden porch by the simple molding, consisting of a fillet around the door, a bolding flowing cyma next to that and a small quarter-round on the outside*

*This carved sandstone Tudor door derives its character from the quality of the moldings and their arrangement. Its air of strength is due to the juxtaposition of light and shade created by its vigorous molding members*

*Although different kinds of moldings create the fireplace frame and the overmantel in this living room, the variation gives it a pleasant character. They are robust and in scale with the exposed beams*

*The moldings about this fireplace are in two groups—a narrow inner bead and an outer, larger bead, both of which give accent to the composition. The beading dominates the other moldings*

*An apartment living room otherwise lacking in architectural interest was transformed by a fireplace faced with brass and studded with nails and surrounded by an architectural frame consisting of two series of stock moldings*

Both the porch and the chimneys of this house at St. Martins, Pa., are made effective by a careful disposition of moldings. They create shade and are a relief to the flat surface of the wall

The simplest form of paneling a room is to apply molding to the wall either directly over the plaster or over canvas laid on the plaster. The shadows of the molding add to the wall's richness

Fillet    Quarter-round

Bead    Cyma reversa

Torus    Cyma recta

Scotia    Cavetto

The profiles of the main molding members are shown above. These members are combined to make various molding patterns

 Echinus    Quarter-round

 Scotia    Cavetto

 Cyma recta    Cyma reversa with fillet above

 Cyma reversa    Torus

The perspectives of molding show how the fillet is used as a finish or transition between combined members

AN OUTLINE OF MOLDINGS

Gillies

## THE GABLE END

*The stucco house above with its interesting gable
treatment at one end is in Riverdale, N. Y., the home
of Robert M. Haig. Julius Gregory was the architect*

The front rooms of these English cottages at Broadway, Worcestershire, are increased in area and light by the bays alongside the doors beneath a long pent roof

In the center picture, taken in the west of England, the smallness of the bay window gives no idea of the amount of cheerful sunlight it admits to the interior within

This corbelled type of bay is, through precedent, in character with the house of half-timber construction. Moot Hall, in Sudbury, Suffolk, furnishes this fine and authentic English example

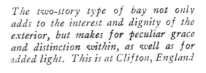

The two-story type of bay not only adds to the interest and dignity of the exterior, but makes for peculiar grace and distinction within, as well as for added light. This is at Clifton, England

THE BAY WINDOW

AN ARCHITECTURAL

LEGACY from ENGLAND

## SMALL AND LARGE
## BAY WINDOWS

*The graceful dignity of this simple bay window is a credit to the English Regency period in which it was designed. In both proportion and detail it is gracious and restrained. The house is in Clifton, England*

*(Below) A house in Sheep Street, Chipping Campden, England, is graced by this small bay which was remodeled from a mullioned Tudor window. It adds to the exterior a pleasant air of domesticity within*

*The early mullioned form of stone bay is the original from which many later varieties have been developed. It is characteristic of Scholastic Gothic and Tudor buildings, such as this Priory, at Chipping Campden*

*The use of a pent-roof connecting twin bays provides a practical shelter for the door, and also gives unity to the design of the house-front as a composition. This house is located in Pershore, Worcestershire, England*

# FOR HOUSES
# IN AMERICA

All these types of bay windows can readily be transplanted to American architecture. Here, for example, is the shallow bay on a modern house at Port Washington, L. I. Wessley Ressell, architect

(Below) This ample bay window has replaced a single window like the one above it, with an obvious gain of light and space within. It is a later addition to an old house in Chipping Campden, Gloucestershire

In this early 19th Century house in Bedfordshire, England, the second-floor drawing room is flooded with sunlight from the tall bay, which also conspicuously aids the appearance of the whole exterior of the house

Both floor space and light have been increased in these old houses at Burford, Gloucestershire, England, by the changing of the original mullioned casement windows to simple white, wood-framed bay windows

# DORMERS *from* FRENCH *and* ENGLISH HOUSES

A late 17th Century English brick house to which the sharp-gabled dormers give lightness and emphasize unity that might otherwise have been disturbed by the different spacing in the windows below

The corner of a house in Gloucestershire, England, showing leaded casements used in dormers and the hipped roof construction in their covering. Sides and roofs are of slate

Although these dormers have only a shallow projection from the steep-pitched Mansard roof, they have a decorative value because of the ornamental leadwork enclosing them. The house is at Versailles and was once the residence of Charles and Frances Wilson Huard

Apart from their usefulness, dormers can be a decorative feature, and it is not unusual to find dormers that are not windows at all but merely applied for a decorative purpose, to emphasize the vertical lines of the window openings below them and to enliven the roof

*The unusual feature of the dormers in this Directoire house at St. Nom-la-Bretéche, France, is that the rounded windows are casements. The spandrels are solid and are hid behind the circular trim of the openings. To give variation, the middle window is peaked*

# UNUSUAL DORMER WINDOWS
# FOR THE AMERICAN HOME

*In some old English houses it is not unusual to find dormer windows with glass cheeks. These increase the light entering the room under the roof and can be used for additional ventilation when one of the panes is hinged*

*Although we generally associate Palladian windows with flat façades, you occasionally find a house in England where the Palladian design is applied to a dormer. It is an interesting treatment, adaptable to Georgian types*

*The interesting features of the dormers on this French residence are their shallow projection from the steep Mansard roof, their variety in shape, the use of scrolls for side ornaments and the small wrought-iron balcony in the middle window. The house dates from the time of Louis XIV*

# THE DISTINCTIVE TOUCH OF ADAM

*The influence of the Adam brothers pervaded all parts
of the house—its architecture, its inside finish, its furniture and its decorative accessories. Here a distinctive
Adam touch is found in the delicate iron work and
graceful tent-shaped hood of the entrance portico in an
English house that dates from 1791*

*An old stone house in Gloucester, England, has this picturesque doorway, with fine Ionic columns and open pediment*

*An entrance of delicate simplicity with painted framework is an interesting contrast to the buff stucco walls of the house*

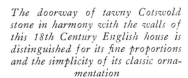

*The doorway of tawny Cotswold stone in harmony with the walls of this 18th Century English house is distinguished for its fine proportions and the simplicity of its classic ornamentation*

*The pent house and Germantown hood are merited revivals of a Colonial style. Adapted here to a modern house, the hood is well placed and beautifully designed. Tooker & Marsh were the architects*

*This severely classic old Annapolis doorway combines with its pure Greek pediment and elaborated Doric columns an unusual decoration of swags on the door-**head***

*An unusual doorway designed by Donn Barber suggests Greek inspiration, with its Doric pilasters and pointed hood. A frame of plaster has inserts of brick*

*The doorway to this house, built in 1690, depends for its distinction upon the hood. It is painted dark brown, the plaster cove white and the wall stucco*

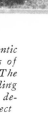

*A sympathetic adaption of a romantic Italian doorway for a modern house is of plaster, molded into decorative effects. The half circle light and the wide molding above make a dignified finish for the design. W. Lawrence Bottomley, architect*

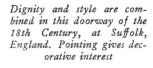

*Dignity and style are combined in this doorway of the 18th Century, at Suffolk, England. Pointing gives decorative interest*

*Great distinction is achieved in the richly designed doorway of the Chase House at Annapolis, Md. The Palladian motif appears in the combination of windows and door, bringing spacious beauty to the entrance*

*This sturdy, well proportioned entrance of the old courthouse at Chester, Pa., is typical of the best 18th Century paneled door*

# IN THE DOOR IS CRYSTALLIZED THE ARCHITECTURE OF THE HOUSE

*In adapting the spirit of the smaller French chateaux to an American house of moderate size the architect, who was Eugene J. Lang, has applied French classic motifs to the entrance door. The effect is dignified and unusual*

*A Colonial design, common to old houses in the United States, consists of a wooden fan over the door and long lights on each side. The door is paneled, or, as in this modern example, of glass. W. Laurence Bottomley, architect*

*The Germantown hood is found in houses of Dutch Colonial and Pennsylvania architecture. A penthouse or projection runs along the façade and over the door is elaborated into an arched hood. Frank J. Forster, architect*

*Inspiration for this door is found in the Palazzo Venezia at Rome—a Baroque window framing above a Classical door. Thus the Italian Renaissance is adapted to an American Italian type house. Lewis Albro, architect*

*This portico entrance is on the wing of a Georgian house and is pronounced harmoniously by a motif adapted from the Georgian—a broken pediment and urn detail. The square columns, of course, are a modern conception. Walker & Gillette, architects*

*The latticed balconies or grilles on this house in Viroflay, France, serve as purely decorative notes of interest and balance*

*(Below) Among the many interesting balconies still to be found in Charleston is this example of wrought iron with a projecting semi-circular bay*

*These balconies of Regency houses at Clifton, England, are so contrived that neither their floor projections nor roofs darken any of the windows. The attenuated pattern of the wrought iron accords with the spirit of design of the period*

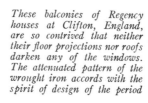

*Balconies of semi-elliptical plan and graceful Regency design give this house front in Cheltenham, England, unusual fascination. They also serve as a protection for the full-length windows*

*The balconies in Charleston, one of the noted architectural marks of that famous city, were executed both in wrought iron and in cast iron. The example shown is of cast iron. It originally had a roof*

The wrought iron balcony gives the one necessary finishing touch to a front of chaste and satisfying composition in this house, La Lanterne, at Versailles

# BALCONIES

### At Times

### A Saving Grace

Just as a sense of humor saves many a difficult situation so a balcony saves many a façade. In the old Read House at New Castle, Del., for example, the note of lightness in the balcony mitigates the austere dignity of the arch doorway below it

Balconies became a vogue over a hundred years ago in England and even cottages sported them. The little square wrought iron balconies on this house at Hampstead supply the only note of frank ornament to the severely plain stucco front

Gillies

*Mr. Forster's successful handling of stone in this chimney recalls Paul Claudel's "Oh, how beautiful is stone, and how soft it is in the hands of the architect! and how right and beautiful a thing is his whole completed work! How faithful is stone, and how well it preserves the idea, and what shadows it makes!"*

# A STONE CHIMNEY BY FRANK J FORSTER, ARCHITECT

# HOW TO BUILD A SMOKELESS FIREPLACE

*The Factors in Building That Assure*

*Success in Burning Coal or Wood*

THE fireplace opening and chimney flue depend on each other, and the size of one must be in proportion to the other. The opening is generally determined before the flue is built, and is governed by the kind of fuel to be burned and the size of the room.

In a moderate size room the width is usually thirty inches to thirty-six inches and the height generally thirty inches. The dimensions vary, however, from thirty inches to sixty inches in width and thirty inches to forty-eight inches in height, the rule being that the height of the opening shall be two-thirds to three-fourths the width. The lower the opening the better the draft, as a higher one permits too much cold air to enter and prevents a good draft. Where this mistake has been made it may be corrected at small expense by a sheet metal shield or hood carried across the top of the opening.

The depth should never be less than one-half the height, two-thirds being better, but never less than sixteen inches for a coal fire nor eighteen inches where wood is burned, twenty inches being better. For a large wood burning fireplace this is made twenty-four inches, but to make it deeper would be poor designing and the heat would not radiate into the room.

The sides in the interior of the fireplace should be run back straight about four inches and then splayed two inches to five inches per foot in depth, so that the opening into the room is wider in front than behind.

The back should be brought upward with a forward slant or a curve, commencing at a point above the hearth. This will tend to contract the fireplace toward the top and insure the air at this important point being thoroughly heated, which greatly improves the draft and causes the heat to be thrown forward and out, rather than upward. At the same time it forms the smoke or back draft shelf above it, without which no fireplace should ever be built, as it prevents and deflects all downward drafts which cause smoke and ashes to be blown into the room.

The throat should be built well to the front of the fireplace and its area should be one to one and one-half times that of the flue. Its width should never be less than three inches nor more than four and one-half inches and its length the entire width

of the fireplace opening. If a patented damper is provided it will govern the size of the throat. When the throat is too wide the air passes up the flue without being warmed first and checks the draft, causing the fire to smoke. The smoke chamber, starting at the top of the throat or damper, should slant about 60° from both sides, until the flue size is reached. The bricks forming the slant in the chamber should be chipped or laid so as to present a smooth surface.

The flue should be led off directly above the center of the smoke chamber. If this is not done the draft will be strongest on the side nearest the flue and the fire likely smoke on the other. When diverting the

vertical direction of the flue on its course up through the building, in order to insure a good draft, it should turn at an angle of 60° and never less than 45°. The steeper the angle the less possibility for soot and ashes to form a deposit and clog the flue.

To eliminate the danger of fire each fireplace should have its own separate flue, lined with terra cotta flue lining for its entire height, built in when the chimney is being constructed. No more than two flues are permitted in the same chimney.

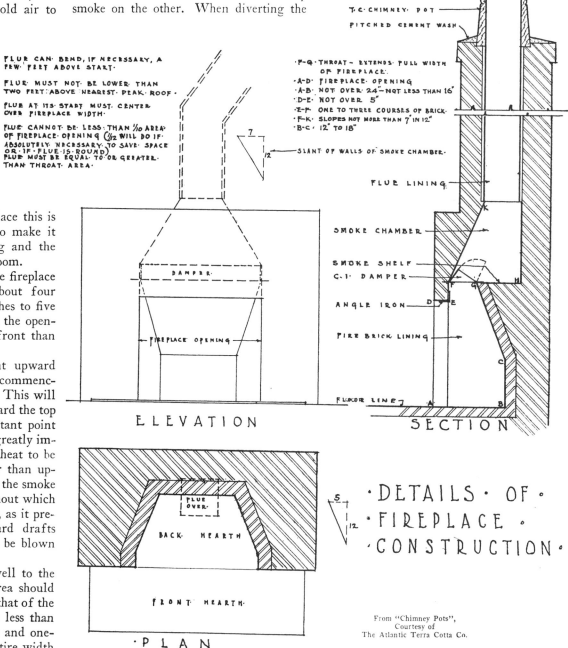

FLUE CAN BEND, IF NECESSARY, A FEW FEET ABOVE START.

FLUE MUST NOT BE LOWER THAN TWO FEET ABOVE NEAREST PEAK ROOF.

FLUE AT ITS START MUST CENTER OVER FIREPLACE WIDTH.

FLUE CANNOT BE LESS THAN 1/10 AREA OF FIREPLACE OPENING (1/12 WILL DO IF ABSOLUTELY NECESSARY TO SAVE SPACE OR IF FLUE IS ROUND) FLUE MUST BE EQUAL TO OR GREATER THAN THROAT AREA.

·F-G· THROAT - EXTENDS FULL WIDTH OF FIREPLACE·
·A-D· FIREPLACE OPENING
·A-B· NOT OVER 24"-NOT LESS THAN 16"
·D-E· NOT OVER 5"
·E-F· ONE TO THREE COURSES OF BRICK·
·F-K· SLOPES NOT MORE THAN 7" IN 12"
·B-C· 12" TO 18"

SLANT OF WALLS OF SMOKE CHAMBER·

T.C. CHIMNEY POT

PITCHED CEMENT WASH

FLUE LINING

SMOKE CHAMBER

SMOKE SHELF

C.I. DAMPER

ANGLE IRON

FIRE BRICK LINING

FLOOR LINE

DAMPER

FIREPLACE OPENING

ELEVATION

SECTION

FLUE OVER

BACK HEARTH

FRONT HEARTH

·PLAN·

·DETAILS· OF·
·FIREPLACE·
·CONSTRUCTION·

From "Chimney Pots",
Courtesy of
The Atlantic Terra Cotta Co.

The Tudor atmosphere is crystallized in the stone surrounds, paneled chimney breast and carved pilasters of this fireplace in the home of Leland H. Ross, Madison, N. J. F. G. Behr and O. B. Smith, architects

(Below) The Elizabethan paneling and furniture in this bedroom of an English country house are fittingly accompanied by a high stone fireplace with a shallow overmantel paneling of the period. Richardson & Gill, decorators

An unusual fireplace, found in the New York City home of Clayton Sedgwick Cooper, consists of a black plaster chimney breast sunk into the white wall and decorated with a bronze insert. Dwight James Baum, architect

# FIREPLACES
## *of*
## PERIOD DESIGN

In a remodeled farmhouse one may well preserve the sturdy old fireplaces. This was done in the home of Webb W. Wilks at New Canaan, Ct. The great fireplace beam and Dutch oven are features

An authentic Colonial design, in the home of Lawrence M. Keeler, Whitinsville, Mass., is unusual for the wide opening of the fireplace. The simplicity of its lines are commendable. Joseph D. Leland, architect

The supporting stone columns, carved wood mantelshelf and fireback in herringbone brick pattern make this a distinguished fireplace for a Tudor room of large proportions. Walker & Gillette, architects

Carved wood decorations, swags of game, fruit and flowers, in the manner of Grinling Gibbons surround the overmantel panel in one of the rooms of the home of Leland H. Ross at Madison, N. J.

*In a wide hall of Colonial design double stairs are effective. A door opens between them, with a closet on each side*

# THE DIFFERENCE IN STAIRS

*Ease is given the stairs shown below by the landing and the flight that goes up over the door. The handrail is mahogany and the other wood painted flat Colonial white*

*The treatment of this handrail in an old English house is worthy of emulation here. The woodwork is oak pegged together*

*Dog gates were a picturesque and practical feature of old English stairways and might be adopted here, to keep Towser where he belongs*

*A detailed view of this old English staircase*

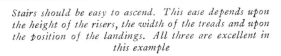

Stairs should be easy to ascend. This ease depends upon the height of the risers, the width of the treads and upon the position of the landings. All three are excellent in this example

Harmony between the curve of this handrail and the slim wrought iron of which it is made has created a stairway of beauty. Its angle also solves the problem of limited space in a re-modeled city house. The inner handrail is a prac-tical idea. Butler & Corse, architects

Curved free standing stairs or stairs supported on only one side have an undeniable lightness and grace. In this example from a New York house the stone steps are sur-mounted by a wrought iron balustrade and rail-ing of great delicacy. William F. Dominick, architect

Where space permits, the stairs can be confined in a special "well," set apart from the hallway. This distinction is necessary in some houses. Here it is used in a small house, the stairs being finished with mahogany treads and handrail. A wide landing is created by the turn of the stairs. Dwight James Baum, architect

*In the English type of house the supporting roof timbers are often exposed. The space between the timbers is plastered in the same manner as the walls. The architects of this were Peabody, Wilson & Brown*

THE

DECORATIVE

CEILING

*In houses of Italian precedents the supporting floor beams are exposed and the space between paneled. This style was adopted for the home of A. J. Thomas, architect, at Hartsdale, N. Y.*

*A decorative coved ceiling has been created in this residence, the home of W. J. Brainard, Scarsdale, N. Y., by heavy moldings placed to form regular panels. A. J. Bodker, architect*

*Geometric patterns worked in plaster is the contemporaneous ceiling for Jacobean rooms. Here it has been used in the home of W. M. Wickes, near Baltimore, Md. Smith & May, architects*

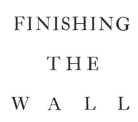

FINISHING

THE

WALL

*It is the interior of this type to which rough texture plaster wall finishes are especially suited, to which, in fact, they are a means of complete architectural expression. Bloodgood Tuttle, architect*

*Among the patented wall finishes is this type, in cement, designed for a formal foyer or lobby and closely imitating the famous Caen stone of Normany*

*There is an open grained stone called Travertine; its imitation is shown here, in a cement finish that reproduces the Travertine effect almost to perfection*

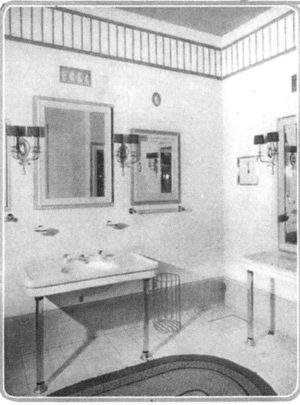

*This type of English plastered interior demands a roughly textured wall for the rendering of its true handiworked character*

*Tile is the ideal finish for bathroom walls. Here the white tiles are relieved by blue and white Wedgwood placques and a blue border*

*No better wall surface than tiles is possible in a kitchen. The simple borders around window and door give sparkle to these walls*

# COLORS TO PAINT THE HOUSE

## SUGGESTIONS FOR VARIOUS STYLES

### COTTAGE TYPE

| | | | |
|---|---|---|---|
| *Body* | Silver Gray | *Body* | Ivory |
| *Roof* | Red-Brown | *Roof* | Red-Brown |
| *Cornice, Corner Boards, Etc.* | Ivory | *Cornice, Corner Boards, Etc.* | Ivory |
| *Sash* | Ivory | *Sash* | Ivory |
| *Front Door* | Ivory | *Front Door* | Ivory |
| *Body* | White | *Body* | Colonial Yellow |
| *Roof* | Moss Green | *Roof* | Moss Green |
| *Cornice, Corner Boards, Etc.* | White | *Cornice, Corner Boards, Etc.* | Ivory |
| *Sash* | White | *Sash* | Bottle Green |
| *Blinds* | Moss Green | *Front Door* | Ivory |

### BUNGALOW TYPE

| | | | |
|---|---|---|---|
| *Body* | Seal Brown | *Body* | Cream |
| *Roof* | Venetian Red | *Roof* | Red-Brown |
| *Cornice, Corner Boards, Etc.* | | *Cornice, Corner Boards, Etc.* | |
| | White (or Ivory) | | Cream |
| *Sash* | White (or Ivory) | *Sash* | Cream |
| *Body* | Ivory | *Body* | Silver Gray |
| *Roof* | Weathered Brown | *Roof* | Moss Green |
| *Cornice, Corner Boards, Etc.* | | *Cornice, Corner Boards, Etc.* | |
| | Sage Green | | Silver Gray |
| *Sash* | Sage Green | *Sash* | Moss Green |

### THE MONGREL AMERICAN

| | | | |
|---|---|---|---|
| *Body* | Colonial Yellow | *Body* | Ivory |
| *Cornice, Corner Boards, Etc.* | Ivory | *Cornice, Corner Boards, Etc.* | Ivory |
| *Roof* | Weathered Brown | *Roof* | Silver Gray |
| *Other Shingled Surfaces* | Ivy Green | *Other Shingled Surfaces* | Sage Green |
| *Sash* | Bottle Green | *Sash* | Sage Green |
| *Body* | Pearl Gray | *Body* | Ivory |
| *Cornice, Corner Boards, Etc.* | White | *Cornice, Etc.* | Rich Dark Brown |
| *Roof* | Weathered Brown | *Roof* | Weathered Brown |
| *Other Shingled Surfaces* | Moss Green | *Other Shingled Surfaces* | Ivy Green |
| *Sash* | Black | *Sash* | Bottle Green |

### THE COLONIAL TYPE

| | | | |
|---|---|---|---|
| *Body* | Colonial Yellow | *Sash* | Bottle Green |
| *Roof* | Red-Brown | *Front Door* | Brown Oak |
| *Cornice, Corner Boards, Etc.* | White | *Body* | White |
| *Sash* | White | *Roof* | Weathered Brown |
| *Front Door* | White Enamel | *Cornice, Corner Boards, Etc.* | White |
| *Body* | Colonial Yellow | *Sash* | White |
| *Roof* | Moss Green | *Blinds* | Moss Green |
| *Cornice, Corner Boards, Etc.* | Ivory | *Front Door* | White |

# FACTS ABOUT PAINTS, STAINS AND VARNISH

*Things You Should Know Before Applying Any of
These Mixtures, and Why You Should Know Them*

OUT of doors painting is best done about mid-spring, and the next best time is early fall. In the spring the air is drier and the temperature most conducive to good results. In late spring, many flies and other small flying things are likely to stick to the wet paint and mar its surface.

Paint thickens quickly in cold weather and is apt to crackle with hair lines not long after it is laid on, or will even tend to flake before it is old. Winter painting, therefore, is inadvisable. Paint put on in summer, on the other hand, is often blistered and drawn by the sun's heat before it is thoroughly dry. In autumn, the season remaining to be considered, the air is damper than in spring, paint takes longer to dry, and must often be helped by adding a considerable quantity of drier to the paint mixture.

Before painting anew, burn off the old surface to be painted, wherever the old coat shows blisters, lumps, crackles or roughness, or is at all flaky or loose. Then sandpaper the surface smooth.

THREE good coats of paint are necessary for new wood out of doors. Allow each coat to dry thoroughly before putting on the next. Two good coats will be sufficient on wood previously painted and whose texture is consequently "filled".

For new wood, the first or priming coat should not be stinted of an ample allowance of white lead which gives body and acts as a filler. Remember that whatever the nature of the first coat, much of it will soak into the wood. For the priming coat on exterior metal surfaces it is advisable to use red lead.

When painting new pine, or other woods in which there is any appreciable residuary sap or resin, shellac the wood before painting. Otherwise the stain from the sap or resin, especially where open grains or pits and knots occur, will eventually show through the paint and produce a brownish stain.

The ground or priming coat, with a good white lead body, should be laid on thick and well brushed out so that no brush marks nor other inequalities of surface occur to roughen later coats.

TO get a good satin finish it is necessary to have a priming coat and three following coats. The second, third and fourth coats, when thoroughly dry, should be rubbed down with powdered pumice stone—not scoured, but rubbed down evenly. Powdered pumice moistened with water tends to produce a higher gloss than when moistened with a little boiled linseed oil. When oil is used for this purpose, care must be taken to use very little so that the body of the paint may not be moved by it.

For a good gloss or enamel finish four coats are necessary after the priming coat has been laid. For a thoroughly good piece of work, these last coats, also, should be rubbed down.

Painted floors, to ensure durable and satisfactory results, should be covered with deck paint that has a surface both hard and elastic, or else given a coat of the dull spar varnish, which possesses the same qualities.

DUTCH COLONIAL TYPES

### 1
| | |
|---|---|
| Body | White |
| Roof | Emerald Green |
| Cornice, Corner Boards, Etc. | White |
| Blinds | Bright Green |
| Sash | White |
| Front Door | Bright Green |

—Green shrubbery to break the hard foundation line, and give further pleasing contrast is very advisable.

### 2
| | |
|---|---|
| Body | Cream |
| Roof | Red-Brown |
| Other Shingled Surfaces | Moss Green |
| Cornice, Corner Boards, Etc. | White |
| Blinds | Moss Green |
| Sash | White |
| Front Door | Walnut Stain |

—Sodded terraces are particularly appropriate with the Dutch Colonial type for all painting plans, but particularly with white and green schemes.

### 3
| | |
|---|---|
| Body | Rich Ivy |
| Roof | Silver Gray |
| Other Shingle Surfaces | Silver Gray |
| Cornice, Corner Boards, Etc. | Rich Ivy |
| Sash | Rich Ivy |
| Front Door | Walnut Stain |

### 4
| | |
|---|---|
| Body | Ivory |
| Roof | Emerald Green |
| Other Shingled Surfaces | Olive Drab |
| Cornice, Corner Boards, Etc. | Ivory |
| Blinds | Olive Drab |
| Sash | Ivory |
| Front Door | Walnut Stain |

THE only valid excuse for staining exterior woodwork is any coloration that may inevitably attend the application of some kind of preservative. Otherwise the weather will achieve, in a short time, more pleasing and durable results than can be produced by artificial means.

To stain new shingles or clapboards a silver gray to match old weathered shingles or clapboards, dip them in a thick, creamy whitewash solution, let them dry, and then fix them in place. The weather will then very soon remove the excess of lime and reduce the new wood to uniform color with the old. The action of the weather may be accelerated by an occasional hosing. This method sounds a bit clumsy but has been employed by able architects with thoroughly satisfactory results where a chemical stain would have produced an ultimate disparity in color.

SPAR varnish for outside unpainted woodwork is a thoroughly weatherproof and durable protective covering. This is the varnish used for exterior ship woodwork—hence the name. It has an amber tinge of its own, besides its high polish, which must be taken into account. A similar dull varnish, with the same kind of tough weatherproof body, can be had when desired.

To remove varnishes from wood, apply wood alcohol to the surface and then wipe off or scrape the loosened varnish. To remove stain apply a solution of oxalic acid or use vinegar. Caustic soda is apt to be too severe and produce burns or excessive bleaching.

Isolated spots or stains on natural wood may be removed by oxalic acid in successive slight applications rather than in one severe application which is apt to result in bleaching too much at one time.

Oil applied to the natural wood emphasizes and brings out the natural contrast and figures of the grain. If the wood is very close-grained, the addition of a little dark powdered pigment to the oil will serve to accentuate the markings.

THE best recipe for natural wood—paneling, architectural trim or furniture—that is to have some kind of dressing is the old English dictum bidding us "feed the wood with oil and polish it with wax." This advice, though intended originally for oak, is equally applicable to other woods. Poppy oil was frequently used in England, but linseed oil does quite as well and is more practicable for common use.

# DECORATIVE HARDWARE
# FOR THE HOUSE

The hardware has much to do with the attractive appearance of a front door. Above is a heavy brass knocker in a graceful shell design, eight inches high. Brass wall lantern wired for electricity and fitted with antique marine glass, fourteen inches high. Brass mail box, twelve inches long with space underneath for newspapers

Frequently one acquires an old piece of furniture with the hardware missing. Above are some excellent reproductions of drawer pulls in antique finished brass that can be used on either reproductions or antiques. Beginning at the top and then reading from left to right—Queen Anne handle four inches wide; Jacobean pull, two and a half inches long; an oval mount suitable for either Hepplewhite or Sheraton furniture, two and a half inches wide; Jacobean, two inches long, and an oval mount with a classic engraved design, two and a half inches wide

The large coat hook above is St. George and the dragon in antique finished brass five and a half inches high. Small brass hook is two inches high

This sturdy Colonial box lock and knob come in heavy brass in an antique finish. There are two sizes, seven by four inches, and four and a half by three and five eighths inches

(Right) Brass drawer pulls, reproductions of authentic English designs. Left to right starting with the top row—Elaborate drop handle. Loop. Round drop with pierced plate. Second row: Engraved knob. Large knob with engraved design and right handle. Small knob. Third row: Loop drop. Oval handle. Small drop

*A decorative chimney iron is a picturesque note of contrast against rough stone, brick or stucco. The graceful S above measures thirty inches long*

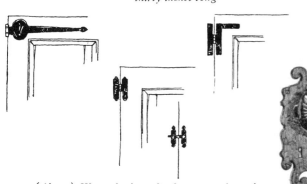

*(Above) Wrought iron hardware consists of a wrought iron hinge, H hinge, H L hinge, and throwover latch with brass knob*

*(Above) Shutter hardware of hand forged iron in rust proof black. The hinge plates on the left shutter are made to fit the blind. L hinges are on the right. Sliding bolt six inches to eight inches long. Ring handle. S shutter hold-back on left blind, eight inches long. Another type on right shutter. Bottom row, reading from left to right: Colonial knob and keyplate in wrought iron or bronze, English Gothic knocker, Colonial door plate, Colonial type bell, and an Italian Renaissance design for bell*

*The hardware enlivens this simple batten doorway. It consists of the thumb latch set, hinge plates, the knocker, the lantern and the foot scraper. All pieces are in hand-forged iron*

*Excellent reproductions of the hardware found in old houses in New England and the South are now available. A beautifully made door set is shown at the left. This consists of L hinges, a thumb latch, lock into which may be inserted a Yale lock, and a ring shaped knocker*

Gillies

# OUTSIDE   THE   FRONT   DOOR

*A fine effect of ruggedness has been given this entrance façade by the use of thoughtfully selected materials. The bricks, for instance, whose unevenness in shape gives such splendid texture and vibrancy to the wall are culls— bricks that have been thrown aside at the yard as imperfect; the lintel is a great oaken beam; the casement sash and door are fashioned of stained oak. Another view of the house is shown on page 129. Mrs. Grace M. Burnham, Great Neck, Long Island, N. Y., is the owner and Frank J. Forster was the architect*

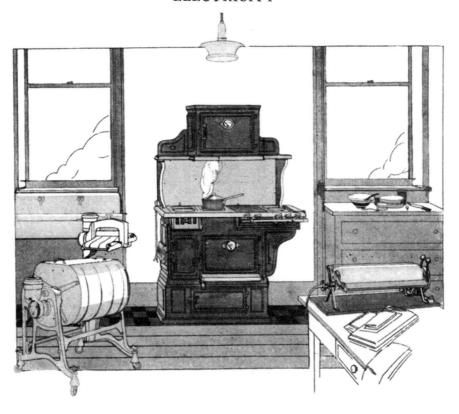

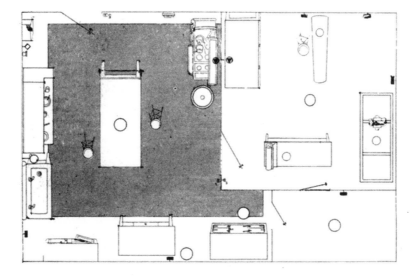

Electrically-run stoves, washing machines and ironers are part of the necessary equipment of the modern house. Provide for them in your house plans. See that enough outlets are furnished in kitchen and laundry

# IN THE

# ELECTRIC

# HOME

On this kitchen and laundry plan there is provision made for an electric wash machine, special lights, servants' annunciator and a three-way entering-room switch. Note the **abundance of outlets**

The electric chart of the living room provides six outlets and a switch as you enter. The furniture is placed in convenient relationship to the electric lights. Side lights and movable lamps are used

In the electrically equipped master's bedroom there should be a switch controlling all lights in the house, a room to room telephone, an outlet for heating coffee and six outlets beside the ceiling light

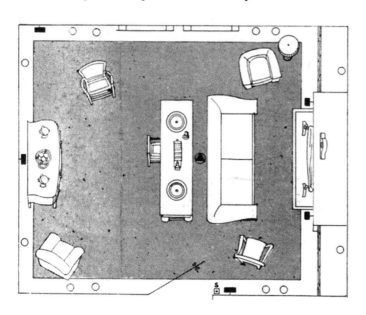

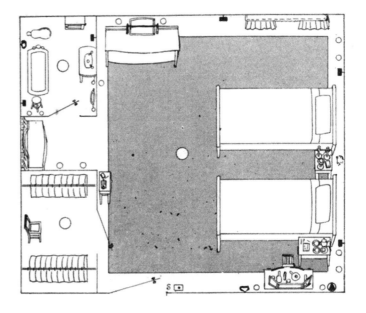

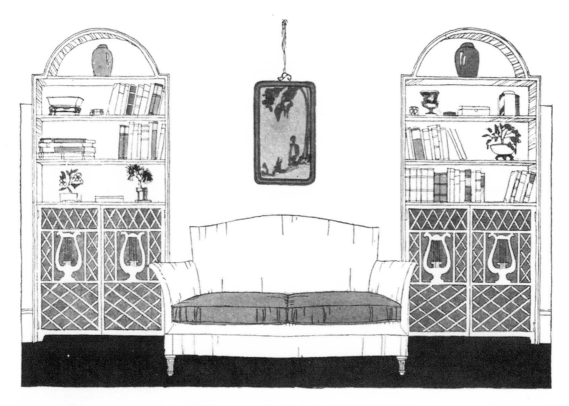

A radiator at the best is an unsightly thing and invariably detracts from the appearance of a room. Placed beneath bookshelves lined with asbestos it may be successfully concealed by a wood lattice with a decorative lyre shaped motif in the center. Designed by Harry C. Richardson

# RADIATOR COVERS

In place of disfiguring the side wall, the radiator in the dining room above is placed in the lower portion of a corner cupboard. The opening at the bottom and the grille above the doors allow for air circulation

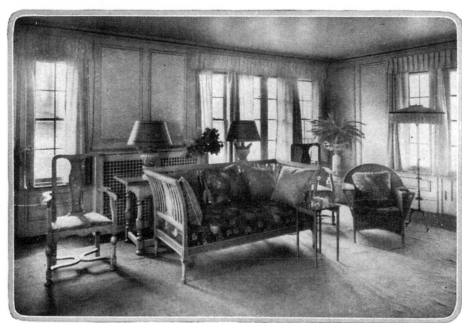

A radiator in a recessed window is concealed with a metal grille and flanked by built-in bookcases. Grilles in bronze, brass or ivory white finish come in square, diagonal and period patterns. Tuttle & Bailey

When a radiator protrudes into the room, as in the sunroom at the left, it is rendered less conspicuous by an enclosure of metal grilles painted the same color as the walls. The top may be used to hold plants

# THE FACTORS IN HEATING A HOUSE

*Heat Losses, the Heater Itself, the Chimney, the Heater's Operation,*
*and Humidity Contribute to Success in Warming the Home*

FIRST—The Heat Losses:

Heat which is lost from any building may be divided into (a) that heat which passes by conduction through the building structure, (b) that heat which is lost due to air infiltration, and (c) that heat which may be lost due to warming air purposely introduced for ventilation. All of these losses increase in direct proportion to the difference in temperature between the inside and outside air. The loss sustained under (b) above is dependent, too, on the tightness of the building structure, especially around doors and windows. Exposed position with reference to strong windows is also a very important point.

Now, the greatest temperature difference which may be expected to prevail at some time during the winter months varies, of course, with the locality, and the home-builder wants to be sure that the plant he installs is sized to meet the maximum requirements. The exact figuring of heat losses is quite a technical problem and most heating contractors use rule of thumb methods which have, through long usage, proven applicable to their particular locality. Such rule of thumb methods are generally so derived that they are always on the safe side and, hence, if lived up to by the heating contractor, will result in safe sizing throughout. Engineering offices in general use a more exact method of figuring heat losses based on very carefully conducted experimental tests.

SECOND—The Heater:

The heater (warm air furnace, steam or water boiler) must be of adequate size, both as to grate area and heating surface for the total heat loss it is to supply. Remember that the firing periods in a house are from 5 to 8 hours apart, depending on the severity of the weather. Be sure, therefore, that the fire pot has sufficient capacity to hold the necessary amount of fuel to carry over this period. Practically all house heaters are rated and fire pots proportioned on the anthracite coal basis for 8-hour firing periods. If, either through necessity or desire, the owner figures on using coke, soft coal or briquetted coal, it will be necessary either to decrease the time between firing periods or select a larger sized heater with proportionally larger firepot. It is for such emergencies as these that the owner should plan. For it is impossible to tell when a change in character of fuel may be necessary. A fire box of more than ample size is the solution.

THIRD—The Chimney:

See that the chimney is of adequate size, both as to cross sectional area and height. Cross sectional area determines the capacity and the height determines the intensity of the draft. Round or square flues are much more efficient than a rectangular flue.

Without a proper sized chimney the best heating system in the world will refuse to function satisfactorily. This trouble always makes itself evident in severe weather just at the time heat is required. To get more heat you must burn more coal. To burn more coal you must supply more air through the fuel bed and dispel greater volumes of the waste products of combustion through the chimney. The chimney should always extend well above the highest ridge of the roof and be located so that the top be not too near any adjacent tall object. Also avoid using a long length of breeching between the heater and the point of connection to the chimney.

Another point to be kept well in mind is the necessity of a chimney design which will eliminate, as far as possible, any fire hazard. It is a matter of record that between 40% and 50% of all the losses in dwelling houses are due either to defective chimney flues, defective connections between heating and cooking apparatus and flues or defective heating, lighting or cooking appliances. Therefore, when the matter of chimney is under consideration, bear the following points in mind:

(1) Build from the ground or basement walls up through the building to point at least 3′ above highest point of roof.

(2) Foundation should be laid on firm ground, using concrete, brick or stone, total area to be not less than twice that of the chimney (outside dimensions).

(3) Use fire clay sleeve jointed flue lining and not sewer tile or terra cotta.

(4) Provide protection for any wood parts of building adjacent chimney walls by means of air space and sheet asbestos board. In no case should any woodwork be built into the chimney.

FOURTH—Operation:

The amount of fuel consumed in heating a home depends on several factors, some of which are within the control of the operator, and some of which are not. A great deal depends on the structure and tightness of the house itself, upon the amount of ventilation desired, etc.

Clean the boiler heating surfaces at regular intervals, using one of the various types of wire brushes supplied for this purpose. Remember that only a slight layer of soot is required on the heating surface to cut down the heat absorption to an alarming degree. A prodigious amount of fuel is wasted annually due to this one factor.

Locate and stop up sources of draft loss. Faulty connections between the sections of the smoke pipe and loose connection between the smoke pipe and the chimney are many times the source of loss, also ill-fitting clean-out doors. These may be made tight with a little fire clay.

FIVE—Humidity:

Artificially heat the air in a room by some direct means, such as a furnace, direct radiation, etc., making no effort to add any moisture, and what is the result? The air in being heated has expanded in volume and the initial moisture content has had to redistribute itself through this expanded volume, resulting in a decrease in the amount of moisture in each cubic foot of air, i.e., decrease in the relative humidity. This heated air, with its low relative moisture content, immediately starts to absorb moisture from everything it touches, with resulting detriment to furniture, plants, etc., and also possibly to your bodily comfort.

It is a well established fact that a room temperature of 65° F., with a relative humidity of about 60%, gives comfort, whereas if the percentage of relative humidity should start to drop, the room temperature remaining the same, the occupant would start to feel the cold in direct proportion to the drop. In other words, the dryer the air at the higher temperatures, the greater the evaporation effect and hence the greater the skin cooling effect. If the percentage of relative humidity should drop to say 25%, then the room temperature, which would be required to give equal comfort to the first condition cited above, would have to be 70° F.

This matter of maintaining a proper degree of humidity in spaces where the air is artificially heated is of prime importance, not only from the standpoint of comfort to the individual, but also from the standpoint of health, as it has been pretty conclusively proven that many of the nose and throat infections get their start from dry air conditions. We have all heard the phrase, "dry as the Sahara." The literal truth is that in most cases our homes and offices are even *dryer* than a desert throughout the months of the year when artificial heating is required. It is enough to say that the average humidity in the Sahara Desert is 15%.

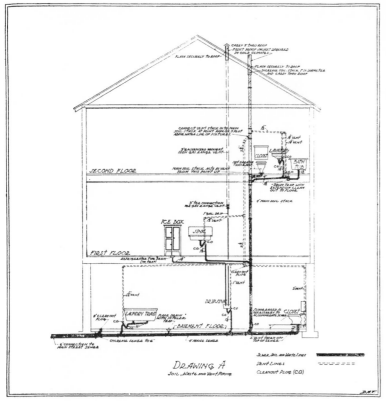

*The drainage pipe system is designed to meet the requirements of the average two-story and basement house. It will be noted that the waste from every fixture must pass through a trap which precludes any back flow of unpleasant odors*

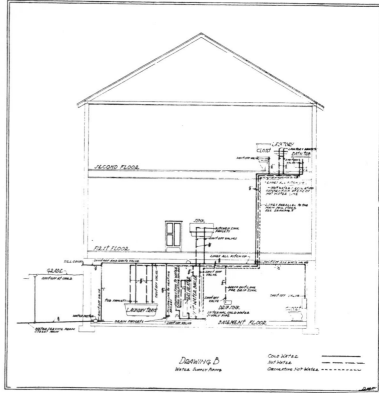

*The supply pipes and fixtures are shown here in cross-section. Shut-off valves are placed near each individual outlet to facilitate any local repairs that may become necessary. Similar provision is made on the main supply lines*

# THE PRINCIPLES

## OF

## PROPER PLUMBING

TO the average layman, the ways and wherefores of plumbing are more or less a mystery. Therefore, to help describe a plumbing system in its simplest form, note the two drawings. Drawing "A" shows the system of drain piping, together with the vents from same, and "B" the system of water supply.

The number of fixtures indicated are what would ordinarily be found in the average small home. On the second floor is the standard bathroom group of closet, tub and lavatory. The first floor shows kitchen sink and separate refrigerator drain. In the basement laundry tubs, floor drain, closet and water heating equipment. As the size of the home increases, so, too, do the number of bath and toilet rooms and the variety of fixtures.

Returning to drawing "A", note that the waste from each fixture must pass through a trap before flowing to the sewer. This trap is located either within the fixture itself, as for example, a water closet, or in the waste line directly adjacent to the fixture, and is vented to atmosphere through a vent pipe connected in, at or near the trap on the sewer side. The trap is there for one purpose only: the prevention of sewer gas escaping into the room. The vent is there for two distinct reasons: first, to prevent syphonage and consequent loss of water seal in the trap of one fixture due to the suction effect caused by the wasting of water from another fixture into the same waste line; and second, to provide a continuous circulation of air throughout the

system of waste piping, thereby eliminating as far as possible excessively foul gas accumulations in any part of the system.

The size of the main house sewer is 4 inches up to the point where it leaves the building, where ordinance generally requires the size to be increased to 6 inches for the remainder of run to cesspool or main street sewer connection. The various waste lines from floor drains, tubs, etc., and the main 4 inch soil stack connect into the 4 inch house sewer at various points within the building. The size of the main soil stack which receives the discharge from water closets on the upper floors is also 4 inches and continues 4 inch through the roof, the opening in the latter being permanently weather proofed with copper flashing.

Cleanouts should be placed in the main house sewer at that point where it leaves the building and also at each point where a change in direction of run occurs, in order that each straight piece of run may be cleaned of obstructions which may occur. Where the sewer line is below the floor level, cleanout connections should be brought up flush with the finished floor. Cleanouts should also be placed in each vent pipe adjacent point of connection to trap or waste

line. Under conditions of actual installation practically all waste and vent piping is effectively concealed in partitions and floor construction. The cleanout connections should be brought through the walls or floor, as the case may be, and terminate in neat nickel plated brass screw caps or plugs set flush with the finished wall or floor.

Now look at drawing "B", showing the system of water supply. First, we have the connection into the building from the street main with curb shut-off valve and box at about the sidewalk or street curb line, as required by practically all ordinances. The water meter is located directly adjacent to the point where the pipe enters the building with connections on both sides of meter valves. From the meter the water service connects to water main at basement ceiling and thence to all plumbing fixtures. The hot water line starts at the top of the hot water tank and parallels the cold water piping and the fixture connections, the pitch of run always being up so as to insure natural circulatory flow.

A well designed system will always include a return circulation line from the ends of the long hot water pipe runs, this return line being carried back to the hot water tank and connected so that when no hot water is being drawn there will be a constant gravity circulation throughout the hot water pipes. This insures hot water in the hot water pipes at points adjacent to the various fixture connections at all times as long as there is hot water in the tank.

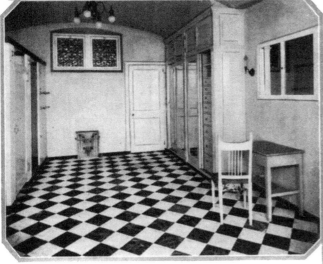

(Below) In the shower room white marble is used for the walls of the showers, bathtub and steam bath, with a contrasting line of black marble for baseboard and top trim. These three types of baths make a very complete equipment for a country house

(Above) One of the baths en suite is equipped with a needle shower encased in glass. The floor of this shower and the wash basin are in marble with gilt bronze mounts. Paneled walls and ceiling and wall fixtures add decorative dignity to the equipment of this bath

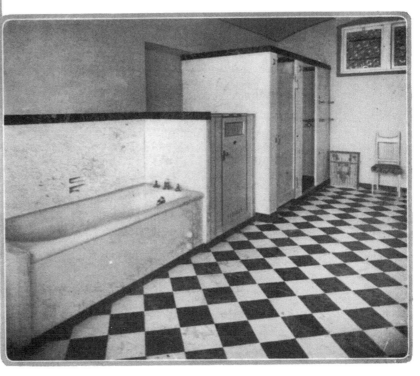

In the residence of W. R. Coe, at Oyster Bay, L. I., are two baths, among many, equipped with all those luxurious necessities that our manufacturers and designers create. In one of the shower rooms the floor is black and white marble. Towel closets range down one side. Walker & Gillette, architects

# L U X U R Y
# I N   T H E   M O D E R N
# B A T H R O O M

In this characteristic bit of Georgian architecture one of the most important elements is the Palladian window, adapted from that most famous motif of the Italian Renaissance. The Cornice, Tympanum and Pediment are architectural forms which may be found on any building with classical antecedents

This Georgian doorway, based on the Roman Doric Order, contains many of the significant features of the classical portico. The Entasis of a column is the slight swelling, greatest about one-third the way up, without which the sides of the column would appear hollow

Casement Window

The various parts of a staircase are so aptly named that one should experience no difficulty whatever in remembering them. What could the Tread be but the Tread, the Riser but the Riser, or what else the Nosing?

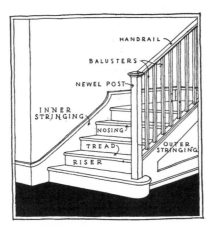

The two most usual types of windows are the casement and the double-hung. One swings on hinges, and the sashes of the other slide up and down in grooves with the aid of concealed weights. The named parts are the same in each

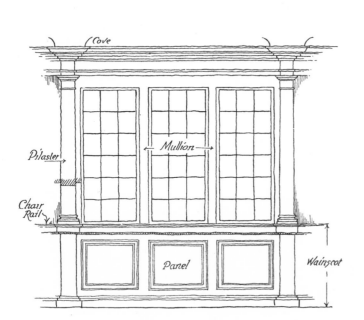

A view of three casement windows from the interior of a formally treated room shows many of those parts of the wall's construction and ornaments whose names are often in doubt. Just below the Cove is the Cornice Moulding

# SOME ARCHITECTURAL TERMS EXPLAINED

# WHAT THE ARCHITECT CHARGES

THE American Institute of Architects, which is the official organization of the profession, has prepared an outline of the professional practice of architects and a schedule of the minimum proper charges for their services. For anyone unfamiliar with all the various phases of an architect's work and his method of arriving at a fair charge for the same, these excerpts from the Institute schedule should be of interest.

The architect's professional services consist of the necessary conferences, the preparation of preliminary studies, working drawings, specifications, large scale and full-size detail drawings, and of the general direction and supervision of the work. The minimum charge for these services, based upon the total cost of the work, is six percent.

On residential work, on alterations, on furniture, decoration and landscape architecture, a higher charge is proper. Thus, on private dwellings a charge of ten percent on the first $50,000, and 8 percent on the balance of cost, is a minimum rate.

The proper minimum rate for landscape architecture is ten percent, and for the designing of fabrics, furniture, fixtures and decoration, fifteen percent. For articles not designed by the architect but purchased under his direction, he is entitled to a charge of six percent.

Payments to the architect are due as his work progresses in the following order: upon completion of preliminary studies, one-fifth of the entire fee; upon completion of specifications and working drawings (exclusive of details), two-fifths additional, the remainder being due from time to time in proportion to the amount of service rendered.

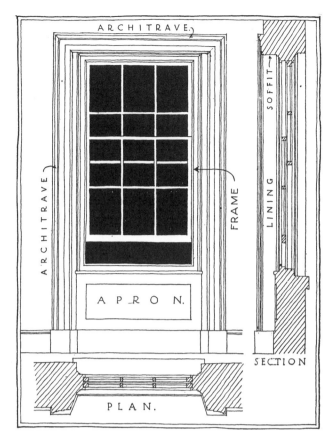

*This plan of a double hung window will show what a variety of architectural elements go into its making. The "apron" is sometimes referred to as the "panel" if this space is paneled*

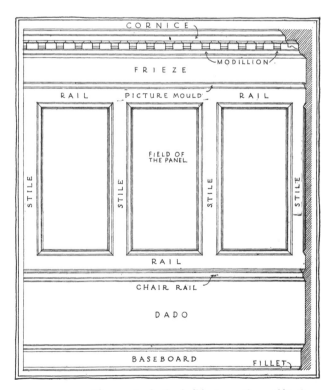

*If you speak the builder's or the architect's language your orders to them will be better understood. Here are a number of technical paneled wall terms that you will be using*

*This sketch combines the essential architectural features to be found in the modern doorway. Other terms are explained on the opposite page by graphic examples*

# CATALOGS FOR THE HOME BUILDER

BRICK

*The Story of Brick; Face Brick Bungalow Small House Plans; The Home of Beauty; The Home Fires; A New House For the Old; English Precedent for Modern Brickwork.*, The American Face Brick Ass'n, 1721 Peoples Life Bldg., Chicago, Illinois.

*Booklet* by Fisk & Co., Inc., New York

*Skintled Brick Work; The Home You Can Afford; Your Next Home*—The Common Brick Manufacturers Ass'n of America, 2128 Guarantee Title Bldg., Cleveland, Ohio.

CEMENT

*A Series of Booklets by* Lehigh Cement Co., Allentown, Pa.

*A Series of Booklets* by The Atlas Portland Cement Co., 25 Broadway, N. Y. C.

*Booklet* by The Sandusky Cement Co., Cleveland, Ohio.

CLOSETS

*Beautiful Clothes Closets*—Knape & Vogt, Grand Rapids, Mich.

FENCES

*Pamphlet* by The Anchor Post Iron Works, 52 Church Street, N. Y. C.

*Landscape Beauty Hints*, Garden Craft Dept., Crystal Lake, Ill.

*Catalog 13*—J. W. Fiske Iron Works, 80 Park Pl., N. Y. C.

*Booklet* by Hartman Sanders, 2155 Elston Ave., Chicago, Ill.

*Lawn Fences That Protect & Beautify*—Pittsburgh Steel Co., 752 Union Trust Bldg., Pittsburgh, Pa.

*Woven Wood Fences*—Robert C. Reeves Co., 187 Water St., N. Y. C.

*Book of Design*—Stewart Iron Works, Cincinnati, Ohio..

*Catalog C, Iron Fence Designs; Special Bulletin of Chainlink Designs*—The Stewart Iron Works Company, Inc., 422 Stewart Block, Cincinnati, Ohio.

*Booklet No. 76B*—Buffalo Wire Works Co., Inc., 475 Terrace, Buffalo, N. Y.

*Booklets* by Wickwire Spencer Steel Corporation, Worcester, Mass.

*Catalogs*—Cyclone Fence Company, Cleveland, Ohio.

FIREPLACES

*Booklet* by Arnold & North, Inc., 124 E. 41st St., N. Y. C.

*Everything for the Fireplace*—Colonial Fireplace Co., 4619 Roosevelt Rd., Chicago, Ill.

*Wood Mantels*—Edwin A. Jackson & Bro., Inc., 50 Beekman St., N. Y. C.

*Series of Booklets* by Arthur Todhunter, Inc., 414 Madison Ave., N. Y. C.

*Furnishings for the Fireplace.* Chattanooga Roofing & Foundry Co., Chattanooga, Tenn.

*The Donley Book of Fireplaces.* Donley Bros. Co., 13943 Miles Ave., Cleveland, Ohio.

*Radiantfire.* General Gas Light Company, Kalamazoo, Mich.

*Booklet* by W. Irving Forge, Inc., 425 Madison Ave., N. Y. C.

*Fireplace Metal Work.* Edwin A. Jackson & Bros., Inc., 50 Beekman St., N. Y. C.

FLOORING

*The Overlooked Beauty-Spots in Your Home.* Arkansas Oak Flooring Co., Pine Bluff, Ark.

*Armstrong's Linoleum Floors.* Armstrong Cork Co., Lancaster, Pa.

*Linotile Floors & Cork Tile Floors.* The Armstrong Cork & Insulation Co., Pittsburgh, Pa.

*Booklet* by The Congoleum-Nairn Co., New York City.

*The Perfect Floor.* Long-Bell Lumber Co., R. A. Long Bldg., Kansas City, Mo.

*New Floors for Old; Color Harmony in Floors; Long Service from Short Lengths; The Floor Which The Years Will Make Precious; How to Lay & Finish Maple, Beech and Birch Floors; What You Can Do With Wide Face Floorings; A Floor of Captive Sunlight; Why and Where to Use 1½" Face; Floors for Educational Buildings; The Floor for Your Home; Asbestone Flooring Composition.* Franklyn R. Muller, Inc., Waukegan, Ill.

*Concrete Floors.* Portland Cement Ass'n, 347 Madison Ave., N. Y. C.

*Booklet* by Stedman Products Co., So. Braintree, Mass.

*Booklet* by W. M. Ritter Lumber Co., 115 E. Rich St., Columbus, Ohio.

FLOOR CARE

*Booklets* by S. C. Johnson's Son, Dept. H. G. 3, Racine, Wisc.

*Booklet* by The Butcher Polish Co., 245 East State St., Boston, Mass.

*Beautiful Floors, Woodwork & Furniture.* The A. S. Boyle Co., 2116 Dana Ave., Cincinnati, Ohio.

GLASS, PLATE

*The Age of Plate Glass.* Plate Glass Mfrs. of America, First National Bank Bldg., Pittsburgh, Pa.

*Tapestry Glass.* Pittsburgh Plate Glass Co., Frick Bldg., Pittsburgh, Pa.

GREENHOUSES

Lord & Burnham Co., Irvington, N. Y.

Hitchings & Co., Elizabeth, N. J.

Wm. H. Sutton, Jersey City, N. J.

T. J. Callahan Co., Dayton, Ohio.

HARDWARE

*Locksets* for French Doors. P. & F. Corbin, New Britain, Conn.

*Good Buildings Deserve Good Hardware; Hand Forged Hardware.* The Florentine Craftsmen, 45 East 22nd Street, New York City.

*Hand Forged Hardware.* W. Irving Forge, Inc., 425 Madison Ave., N. Y. C.

*Booklet* by The McKinney Mfg. Co., Pittsburgh, Pa.

*Modern Hardware for Your Home.* Richards-Wilcox Mfg. Co., Aurora, Ill.

*Russwin Period Hardware.* Russell & Erwin Mfg. Co., New Britain, Conn.

*The Colonial Book.* Sargent & Co., 31 Water St., New Haven, Conn.

*Booklet on Wrought Iron Hardware*, by Arthur Todhunter, Inc., 414 Madison Ave., N. Y. C.

*Correct Windows for the Home.* The G. F. S. Zimmerman Co., Inc., 1 Broadway, Frederick, Mo.

*Booklet* by Yale & Towne, Stamford, Conn.

HEATING

*Ideal-Arcola Heating Outfit.* American Radiator Co., 40 W. 40th Street, N. Y. C.

*Letters To and Fro.* Burnham Boiler Corporation, Irvington, N. Y.

*Modern Furnace Heating.* Hess Warming and Ventilating Co., 1209 Tacoma Bldg., Chicago, Ill,

*Booklet* by The Kelsey Warm Air Generator, 237 James Street, Syracuse, N. Y.

*Perfect Warm Air Furnaces.* Richardson & Boynton Co., N. Y. C.

*Thatcher Boilers & Thatcher Furnaces.* Thatcher Co., 131 West 35th St., N. Y. C.

*Capitol Boilers.* U. S. Radiator Corp., Detroit, Mich.

*New Facts About Oil Heating.* Williams Oil-O-Matic Heating Corp., Bloomington, Ill.

*Booklet* by EverHot Heater Co., 5219 Wesson Ave., Detroit, Mich.

*The Proper Operation of The Home Heating Plant.* Minneapolis Heat Regulator Co., 2790 Fourth Avenue, So. Minneapolis, Minnesota.

*Booklet* by The Bryant Heater & Mfg. Co., 976 E. 72nd St., Cleveland, Ohio.

HOLLOW TILE

*Natco Homes.* National Fireproofing Co., 1426 Fulton Bldg., Pittsburgh, Pa.

*Book of Hollow Tile Residences.* Hollow Building Tile Ass'n, Conway Bldg., Chicago, Ill.

INCINERATORS

*The Sanitary Elimination of Household Waste.* Kerner Incinerator Co., 1029 Chestnut St., Milwaukee, Wisc.

INSULATION

*Armstrong Corkboard Insulation; Insulation of Dwellings.* Armstrong Cork & Insulation Co., 193-24th Street, Pittsburgh, Pa.

*Booklet* by Samuel Cabot, Inc., 8 Oliver St., Boston, Mass.

*Celotex Insulating Lumber.* Celotex Co., 111 West Washington St., Chiicago, Ill.

*Heat Insulation for Houses.* Flaxlinum Co., St. Paul, Minn.

*Keystone Hair Insulation; Making Comfort an Economy.* Johns-Mansville Co., Madison Ave. & 41st St., N. Y. C.

KITCHEN EQUIPMENT

*Kitchen Units.* Wasmuth-Endicott Co., 1230 Snowden St., Andreus, Ind.

*Booklet* by Janes & Kirtland—133 West 44th Street, N. Y. C.

LATH, METAL

*Hy-Rib and Metal Lath.* Truscon Steel Co., Youngstown, Ohio.

*Building for Permanence & Beauty.* The General Fireproofing Co., Youngstown, Ohio.

LIGHTING FIXTURES

*What Good Taste Decrees in Lamps.* Art Lamp Mfg. Co., 1433 So. Wabash Ave., Chicago, Ill.

*Designs* by Cassidy Co., 101 Park Ave., N. Y. C.

*Booklet* by Luminier Co., 577 Broadway, N. Y. C.

*Booklet* by Edw. N. Riddle Co., Toledo, Ohio.

*Booklet* by Homart Studios, 227 Fulton St., N. Y. C.

*Booklet* by The Horn & Brannon Mfg. Co., 427-435 No. Broad St., Phila., Pa.

*Booklet* by The Handel Co., Meriden, Conn.

*The Decorative Charm of Wrought Iron.* Bozart Lighting Co., Inc., 8 Warren St., N. Y. C.

*Light Outdoors.* Novelty Lamp & Shade Co., 2482 East 22nd St., Cleveland, Ohio.

PAINTS & VARNISHES

*Cabot's Old Virginia White & Tints.* Samuel Cabot, Inc., 141 Milk St., Boston, Mass.

*Booklets* by Devoe & Raynolds Co., 101 Fulton St., N. Y. C.

*Muralite.* M. Ewing Fox & Co., 250 East 136th St., N.Y.C.

*Color Harmony; Handy Book on Painting.* National Lead Co., 111 Broadway, N. Y. C.

*Booklet* by McDougall-Butler Co., Inc., Buffalo, N. Y.

*Booklet* by Martin Varnish Co., Chicago, Ill.

*Booklet* by Berry Bros., Detroit, Mich.

*Booklet* by Valentine & Co., 460—4th Ave., N. Y. C.

PLASTER BASES

*Bishopric For All Time & Clime.* The Bishopric Mfg. Co., 712 Este Ave., Cincinnati, Ohio.

PLUMBING & FIXTURES

*Brass Pipe & Piping.* American Brass Co., Waterbury Conn.

*Homes of Comfort; The New Art of Fine Bathrooms.* Crane Co., 836 So. Michigan Ave., Chicago, Ill.

*Fairfacts Fixtures.* Fairfacts Co., 234 W. 14th St., N. Y. C.

*Maddock Bathrooms.* Thos. Maddock Sons Co., Trenton, New Jersey

*Kohler of Kohler.* The Kohler Co., Kohler, Wisc.

*Speakman Showers & Fixtures.* Speakman Co., Wilmington, Dela.

*Bathrooms of Character.* Trenton Potteries Co., Trenton, N.J.

*Booklet* by Standard Mfg. Co., Pittsburgh, Pa.

PORTABLE HOUSES

*Catalog* by Gorden Van Tine Co., Davenport, Ia.

*Catalog* by E. F. Hodgson Co., 6 E. 39th St., N. Y. C.

*Catalog* by Lewis Mfg. Co., Bay City, Mich.

*Catalog* by Togan Stiles Co., Grand Rapids, Mich.

PUMPS

*Electric House Pumps and Water Supply Systems.* Dayton Pump & Mfg. Co., Dayton, Ohio.

*Running Water in Abundance.* Goulds Mfg. Co., Seneca Falls, N. Y.

RANGES

*Cook With the Gas Turned Off.* Chambers Mfg. Co., Shelbyville, Ind.

*Perfect Cooking Ranges.* Richardson & Boynton, N. Y. C.

*Pamphlet* by George D. Roper Corp., Rockford, Ill.

REFRIGERATORS

*Booklet* by Jewett Refrigerator Co., Buffalo, N. Y.

*Booklet* by Illinois Refrigerator Co., Morrison, Ill.

*Booklet* by Bohn Refrigerator Co., St. Paul, Minn.

*Booklet* by Seegar Refrigerator Co., St. Paul, Minn.

REFRIGERATION

*Booklet* by The Delco-Light Co., Dayton, Ohio. (Dept. P-1)

*Booklet* by The Kelvinator Corp., 2054 West Fort Street, Detroit, Mich.

ROOFING

*Copper—Its Effect Upon Steel for Roofing Tin.* American Sheet & Tin Plate Co., Frick Bldg., Pittsburgh, Pa.

*Olde Stonesfield Roofs & Olde Stonesfield Flagging.* John D. Emack Co., 112 So. 16th St., Phila, Pa.

*Colorblende Book.* Johns-Manville Co., 292 Madison Ave., N. Y. C.

*Booklet* by The Keystone Roofing Mfg. Co., York, Pa.

*Roofing Tile; The Roof Beautiful.* Ludowici-Celadon Co., Chicago, Ill.

*The Roof Everlasting.* Mohawk Asbestos Slate Co., Inc., Utica, N. Y.

*Historic Homes of America.* Red Cedar Shingle Bureau, White Bldg., Seattle, Wash.

*What Color for the Roof.* The Richardson Co., Lockland, O.

*Tudor Stone Roofs.* Rising & Nelson Slate Co., 101 Park Ave., N. Y. C.

*Sheetrock Pyrofill Construction.* U. S. Gypsum Co., 205 West Monroe St., Chicago, Ill.

*Booklet* by The New Jersey Zinc Co., N. Y. C.

*Booklet K-5* by Copper & Brass Research Ass'n., 25 B'way, N. Y. C.

*Buildiing Roofs that Beautify & Last.* American Insulation Co., Roberts Ave. & Stokley St., Phila. Pa.

*Thatched Effect; How to Build a 40-year Roof; Giving The Old House a New Lease on Life.* Creo-Dipt Co., No. Tonawanda, New York.

*Booklet* by Edgecumbe-Newman, Vancouver, Canada.

SCREENS

*Screens That Meet the Test.* The American Brass Co., Waterbury, Conn.

*Screen Your Home in the Higgin Way; Higgin All Metal Window Screens.* The Higgin Mfg. Co., 5th & Washington Ave., Newport, Ky.

SEWAGE DISPOSAL

*Booklet No. 7*, by Aten Sewage Disposal Co., 286 Fifth Ave., N. Y. C.

STONE

*Distinctive Houses of Indiana Limestone.* Indiana Limestone Quarrymen's Ass'n., Box 782, Bedford, Indiana.

STUCCO

*Booklet* by U. S. Gypsum Co., Chicago, Ill.

*Stucco Houses Reinforced with Triangle Mesh Fabric.* American Steel & Wire Co., Chicago, Ill.

TERRA COTTA

*Chimney Pots.* Atlantic Terra Cotta Co., 350 Madison Ave., N. Y. C.

*Color in Architecture.* National Terra Cotta Society, 19 W. 44th St., N. Y. C.

TILE

*Booklet* by Batchelder-Wilson Co., Los Angeles, California.

*Beautiful Tiles.* Associated Tile Mfrs., 831—7th Ave., Beaver Falls, Pa.

WALL BOARD

*Sheetrock Wall Board; Walls of Worth.* U. S. Gypsum Co., 205 W. Monroe St., Chicago, Ill.

WALL COVERINGS

*Sanitas and Its Uses; Sanitas, Modern Wall Covering.* The Standard Textile Products Co., 320 B'way., N. Y. C.

W. H. S. Lloyd Co., 105 West 40th St., N. Y. C.

*Walls & Their Decorations.* Wallpaper Mfrs. Ass'n. of the U. S., 461—8th Ave., N. Y. C.

James Davis, Inc., 1406 Milwaukee Ave., Chicago, Ill.

WATER SOFTENERS

*Bulletin* by The Duro Pump & Mfg. Co., 503 Monument Ave., Dayton, Ohio.

*Permutit.* The Permutit Co., 440 Fourth Ave., N. Y. C.

WEATHER STRIPS

*Booklet* by Chamberlain Metal Weather Strip Co., Detroit, Mich.

*The Diamond Way.* The Diamond Metal Weather Strip Co., Columbus, Ohio.

*Monarch Metal Weather Strip Manual; Only ⅛ of an Inch.* Monarch Metal Products Co., 5020 Penrose St., St. Louis, Mo.

WINDOWS

Detroit Steel Products Co., A-2256 East Grand Boulevard, Detroit, Mich.

*Things You Ought to Know About Casement Windows.* Casement Hardware Co., 220 Pelouze Bldg., Chicago, Ill.

*Crittall Universal Casement.* Crittall Casement Window Co., Detroit, Mich.

*International Casements for Homes of Distinction & Charm.* International Casement Co., Jamestown, N. Y.

WOOD

*Pine Homes.* California White & Sugar Pine Mfrs. Ass'n., 690 Call Bldg., San Francisco, California.

*Better Built Homes.* Curtis Companies Service Bureau, Clinton, Ia.

*Redwood Homes Booklet.* The Pacific Lumber Co., 923 Pershing Sq. Bldg., 100 E. 42nd St., New York City.

*Cypress Colonial Plan Book.* Southern Cypress Mfrs. Ass'n. 1210 Paydras Bldg., New Orleans, La.

*Series of Booklets* by Southern Pine Ass'n., New Orleans, La.

*Pondosa Pine.* Western Pine Mfrs. Ass'n., Portland, Ore.

*Information Sheets* by California White & Sugar Pines Mfrs. Ass'n., 690 Call Bldg., San Francisco, Calif.

*Historic Mahogany.* The Mahogany Ass'n., Inc., 1133 B'way N. Y. C.

*The Story of American Walnut.* American Walnut Mfrs. Ass'n., Rm. 908, 616 So. Mich. Ave., Chicago, Ill.

*Booklet* by The Birch Mfrs. Co., 219 F. R. A. Building, Oshkosh, Wisc.

*Booklet* by Red Cedar Lbr. Mfrs. Ass'n., 4447 White Bldg., Seattle, Wash.

*Beautiful American Gumwood.* Gumwood Service Bureau of The Hardwood Mfrs. Ass'n., Bank of Commerce Bldg., Memphis, Tenn.

WOODWORK

*Keeping Down the Cost of Your Woodwork; Windows for Better Built Homes; Window and Door Frames; Entrance & Exterior Doors; Interior Doors & Trim.* Curtis Service Bureau, Clinton, Iowa.

*Adding Distinction to The Home; Millwork Handbook.* Morgan Sash & Door Co., Chicago, Ill.

WROUGHT IRON

*The Charm of Wrought Iron.* Bozart Lighting Co., 8 Warren St., N. Y. C.

*Booklet* by Florentine Craftsmen, 45 E. 22nd St., N. Y. C.

*Booklet* by W. Irving Forge, Inc., 425 Madison Ave., N.Y.C.

*Booklet* by Arthur Todhunter, Inc., 414 Madison Ave., N.Y.C.

# A PORTFOLIO
# OF SMALL AND LARGE
# HOUSES

*Stone, Brick, Half-Timber, Clapboard, Stucco, and
Shingle Houses with Plans—Garages
and Driveways—Log Cabins*

Wallace

## THE MELLOW QUALITY OF RUBBLE MASONRY

*The neighborhood of Philadelphia is especially fortunate in having a local ledge stone that is easily quarried and, when laid up with wide joints, attains a mellowness of color that is peculiar to this district. An example of this is found in the colors, pattern and surface of the stone work in the home of A. H. Reeve, at Chestnut Hill, Pa. Robert R. McGoodwin was the architect*

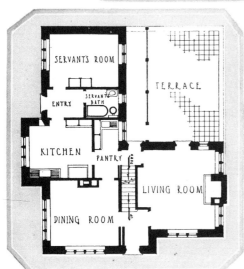

*The Tudor style, generally associated with large country houses, has been successfully developed in this small residence, the home of Frank R. Ford*

# A LITTLE TUDOR HOUSE

# IN ROSELAND, N. J.

MICHAEL STILLMAN, *Architect*

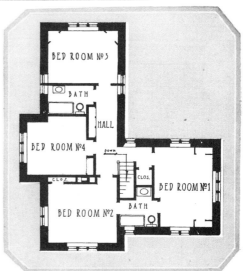

*A larger amount of space than is usually assigned to it is given over to service; on the other hand, the paved terrace is really an outdoor extension of the living room*

*Since the servants are given a room downstairs, the four bedrooms upstairs are for the family. Their arrangement affords an abundance of light and ventilation*

*The scale of the architectural details has been so carefully studied in the exterior that the house is one of rare examples of completely successful architecture*

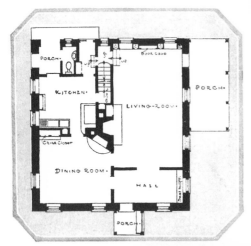

*A small house which is really small, while entirely fulfilling its requirements as a dwelling. Its exterior is thoroughly in character with the local colonial types*

*The details of the porches and shutters follow, with an unusual degree of architectural fidelity, the precedent of early farmhouses in eastern Pennsylvania*

# PENNSYLVANIA

# STONEWORK

*The plans are necessarily compact, yet adequate in the accommodation of a large living room. Conservation of space is the secret of planning so small an area*

*The second floor plan provides a surprising number of bedrooms. The architect is R. Brognard Okie, and the owner, Miss Mary C. Gyger at Bryn Mawr, Pennsylvania*

*The sleeping porch has been contrived in a manner not too incongruous with the early Pennsylvania farmhouse type which was used here as the architect's model*

This house of local stone is built into the grade of a sloping site. An interesting detail is the outline of an heirloom candlestick, utilized for the piercings in the upper panels of the shutters

Melichor

A stone retaining wall, with an attractively designed gate, marks the transition in grade from the lower lawn to the upper portion. This is the home of Kenneth K. Kirwan, Guilford, Baltimore, Md., of which W. H. Emory, Jr., was the architect

Efficiency and economy of plan characterize the interior arrangement of this house. The kitchen and pantry, with maid's room and back stairs are planned with the utmost compactness. The main hall carries through from entrance to garden fronts

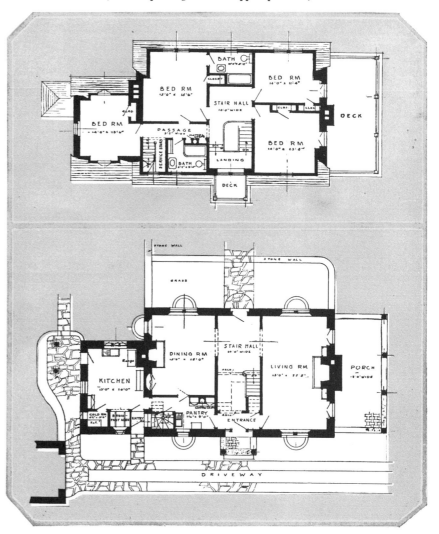

# IN THE
# STONE OF BALTIMORE

*The name of the house is as English as its architecture—Fryars, West Chiltington. Intelligent restoration revealed its beauty. The mellow brickwork of the drip courses and around the windows gives a brighter tone to the somber dignity of the lichen-covered gray stone walls*

*An iron gate of delicate tracery opens on to stone steps leading up to the flagstone pathway, bordered by old-fashioned flowers. The ivy with which the house was smothered has been removed, revealing the delightful proportions of the weathered building*

*In the living room the fine old oak beams of the ceiling are exposed, and floor, doors, and mantelpiece are of oak planks toned dark with age. The original fireplace was brought to light, and a beautiful fireback has been installed*

AN

OLD SUSSEX

HOUSE

RESTORED

Van Anda

Among the buildings on the estate of
Richard Sellers, at Belle-
vue, Delaware, is this cottage of whitewashed
stone in the English style. The
roof is of green and purple slate

The open porch on the kitchen wing
is a detail native to the more southern sections of the United States

The entrance, quite ornate in design, is of limestone, the door being
of oak panels in natural finish

There is practically
no hall. The dining
room and kitchen
make one large
room, with the liv-
ing room on the
other side

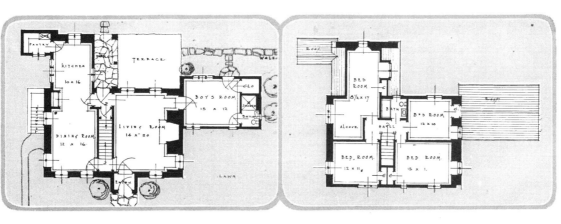

Four bedrooms and
a bath on the sec-
ond floor make this
quite a commodious
house. The archi-
tect was Prentice
Sanger

Gillies

# A HOUSE THAT HUGS

## A HILLTOP

*Charles L. Wren, Owner*
*South Norwalk, Conn.*

### FRANK J. FORSTER , *Architect*

*At the opposite end of the living room from the combination door and casement stands this sturdy fireplace with its exposed stone chimney*

*The living room, rough plastered, wide boarded, and lighted by great casements, is in itself the main body of the house and indicates the whole form of this low, delightful building*

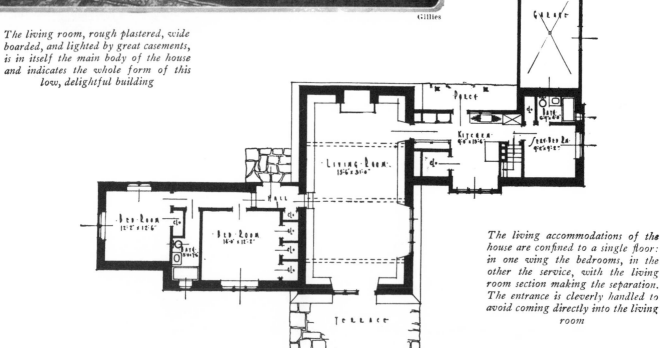

*The living accommodations of the house are confined to a single floor: in one wing the bedrooms, in the other the service, with the living room section making the separation. The entrance is cleverly handled to avoid coming directly into the living room*

Gillies

The view above shows how well the
house has been set into its hilltop
site, with low eaves, sharp gables,
and long roof lines closely moulded
to the contour of the ground

Below can be seen how the walls of
the house rise from the ground in
the stone of the site, making the
building seem almost an integral
part of its setting

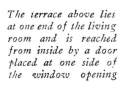

The terrace above lies
at one end of the living
room and is reached
from inside by a door
placed at one side of
the window opening

The entrance doorway,
in its secluded situa-
tion, is marked by a
curve in the eave line
and a simple facing of
gray stucco and timber

Lee

# A  DOOR  OF  CONTRASTS

The Spanish and Italians practised the excellent custom of placing decoration where it was most effective. They concentrated it at certain points and contrasted it with its surroundings. The flat wall suddenly flowered with a richly wrought iron grill. The plain surface abruptly broke out into a doorway of exquisite detail. The same spirit is found in this entrance to the home of C. C. Merritt, at Larchmont, N. Y. Rough walls with simple window openings make interesting façades. A flight of stone stairs expanding at the top to a platform gives approach to the door. Then the door itself, with its richly carved twisted engaged columns

*The door is of heavily paneled oak simply set in its frame as befits the informal rugged character of the entrance approach with its evergreens and rock plants*

*Graystone and rough finished stucco give to the home of J. D. Dithridge at Great Neck, L. I., an interesting mass and detail combined with dignified simplicity*

*Gables give an impression of height. Although a one-story house, the approach of the path and the planting of cedars help to add a sense of size*

# A STONE BUNGALOW

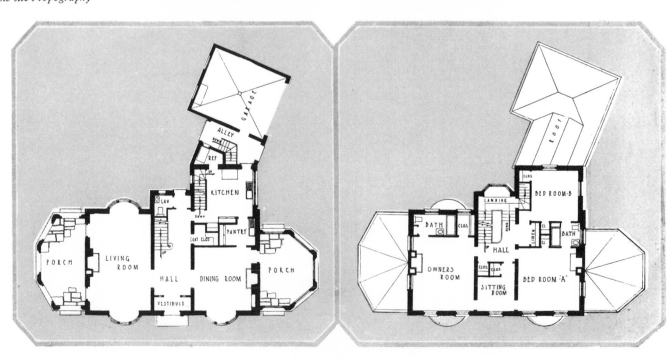

*From Baltimore south to the James River the Georgian spirit pervades most of the Colonial architecture and has come down, naturally, to much of the modern work, as in this house at Guilford, Md., with its fine formality and graceful details*

*The curving bow-windows and the polygonal porches are interesting and attractive features of the house. Its plan shows how these things have combined to make the living room unusually effective. The angle of the garage is due to the site's topography*

# TWO GEORGIAN HOUSES IN BRICK

Lively colors are found in the walls and roof of the home of Fayette Baum, Syracuse, N. Y., both the brick and the slate being variegated. Contrast is found in the white trim and keystones. Dwight James Baum, architect

Entrance to the house is reached through a gate of high brick pillars and wrought iron. Then one comes to this Georgian doorway with its simple columns and arched pediment and its carved over-door panels and trim

Upstairs the plans show the owner's suite of bedroom and bath, a guest room and a well-lighted sewing room. Both upstairs and down this house is suitable and adequate for an elderly couple, as is its purpose

The first floor plan is irregular, the entrance and hall being in one corner with the service behind. The living room and dining room are generously proportioned. French doors lead from the living room to the porch

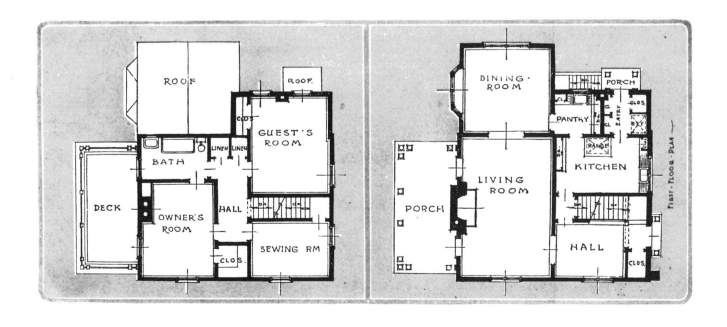

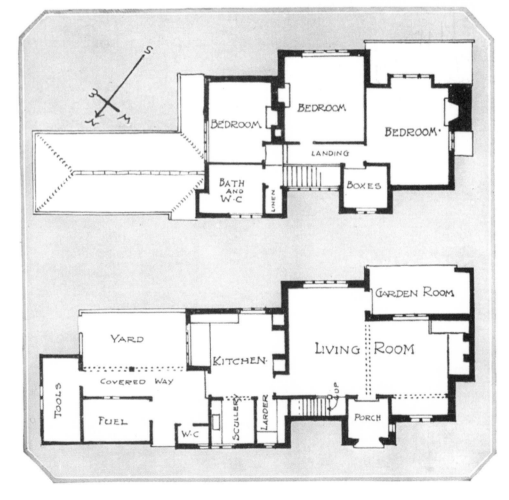

Three hundred years ago Abraham Cowley prayed that he might "a small house and large garden have," and in Bentley Cottage, Great Missenden, England, he would find his wish fulfilled. The site, which was an ordinary grass field, now contains a house, flower and kitchen gardens, lawns, and orchard

A large living room occupies most of the first floor and from the kitchen a covered way leads to fuel and tool sheds. The floors are of oak and the hardware of wrought iron locally made. Upstairs are three bedrooms, each with an open fireplace, a bath and a box room for storage. A. Percival Starkey was the architect

# BRICK  HOUSES
## *in*
# ENGLAND  AND
# AMERICA

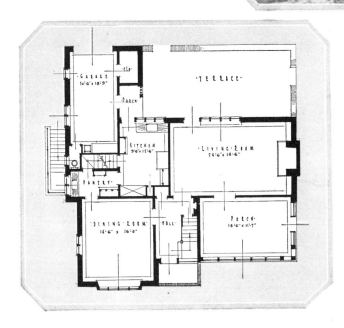

An interesting, but not too-artificial texture
has been accomplished by the skillful use of
clinker-faced brick. The owner is W. Jule
Day, at Douglaston, L. I., and the architect is Frank J. Forster

The plan is ingeniously arranged on a
scheme of three wings, one of which is
utilized to accommodate the garage, which
is conveniently entered through the house
or from the terrace

The walled terrace is entered through a
wrought-iron gate, which contributes its element of craftsmanship to the architectural
craftsmanship of the whole. The vestibule
porch at the end enters the garage

Not a little planning was necessary to ad-
just the requirements to the available floor
area. The hall, necessarily, is a right-an-
gled corridor, but there are five bedrooms,
three baths and a study

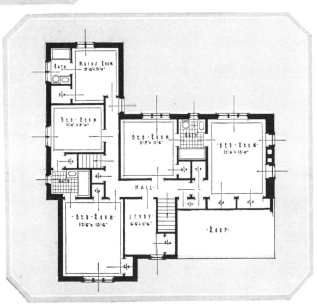

Toloff

# BY GARDEN STAIRS TO THE SECOND FLOOR

*The climate of California does such pleas-
ant things to architecture, with open arcades,
balconies, loggias, and outside stairways,
that the airy style of the lower Coast inevitably seeps inland. Strangely enough, when
it reaches the shores of Lake Michigan, as in*
*this house of Evanston, Illinois, it not only
seems highly appropriate, but brings something fine and fresh to the sterner situation.
Fred P. Warren is the owner and Reginald
Johnson, of Johnson, Kaufmann & Coate,
of Los Angeles, is the architect of the house*

*Elements in the home of J. A. Kienle, Forest Hills, L. I., were drawn from smaller English manor houses. Brick walls are painted a warm gray with the corners laid up in natural colored brick projecting slightly from the main face of the wall. The roof is red tile, surmounted by chimney tops and a dove-cote placed at the intersection of the wings*

*While the doorway is classic in appearance, it is not entirely classic in its details, as can be seen in the molded corners behind the pilasters and the flattened lines of the consoles above. It harmonizes well with its simple environment. Plain casement windows and a bay window with a bright blue roof are other features. W. Laurence Bottomley was the architect*

A VARIATION

OF THE

ENGLISH

STYLE

Collinge

*The simplicity of this front is made interesting by the texture and profile of the shingle roof and the battened shutters*

*The first floor provides most of the accommodation. The service wing and rear are attractively and nicely planned*

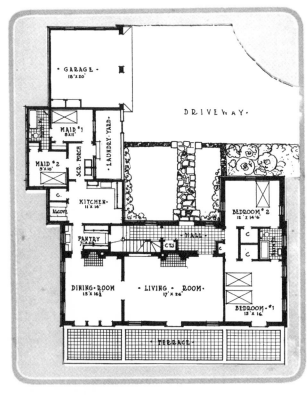

## "LE PETIT MANOIR"
### *Montecito, California*

Collinge

*There is a distinct feeling of the ancient French farm in this California house called suitably "Le Petit Manoir"*

*The second floor plan shows the disposition of the roofs, and also the two bedrooms and bath of the second floor*

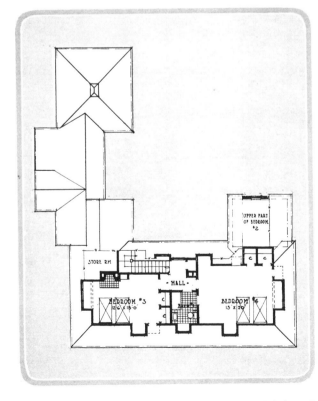

# OF FREDERIC L. BAXTER

*Soule, Murphy and Hastings, Architects*

*From the rear garden the simplicity of the architecture can be seen at a glance. The walls are stucco, the roof shingle. There is sufficient irregularity to the plan to prevent monotony in the façade*

*A long, well lighted gallery traverses the north side of the ground floor, giving access to all the living rooms—the drawing room, library and the dining room. From this the stairs run up in the service wing*

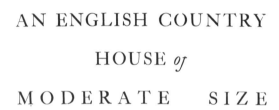

# AN ENGLISH COUNTRY
## HOUSE *of*
## MODERATE SIZE

HARRY REDFERN, *Architect*

*The oblong bay window projected from one corner has casement windows on three sides, giving ample light to the drawing room below and a chamber above. Between this and the ell runs a glass roof porch*

*The drawing room, which commands a garden view through the bay window, is furnished simply, harmonizing with the architecture of the house. It is livable without striving for any especial decorative effects*

This house should prove the assertion that even very small dwellings may have real architectural distinction. Done in what has come to be known as the English Cottage style, it has been appropriately given stuccoed walls, a shingle roof and casement windows

The first floor has been beautifully planned to contain a living room of considerable size, with an alcove at one end for working and one at the other for dining; a servant's room and bath; kitchen, pantry and garage

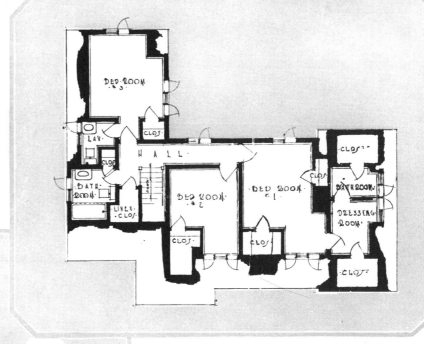

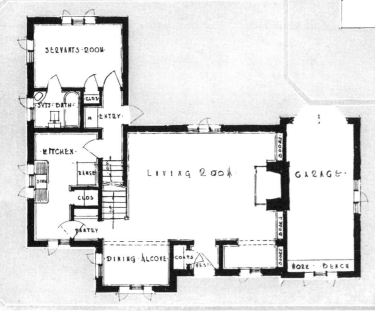

For a house of such modest dimensions an astonishing amount of bedroom, bath, and closet space has been provided. The wall construction is of hollow tile. J. H. Jewett, jr., Bronxville, N. Y., owner; Lewis Bowman, architect

A SMALL STUCCO HOUSE WITH AN INTERESTING PLAN

# AN UNUSUAL ENTRANCE

*The charm of this entrance to the home of Francis Keil at Scarsdale, N. Y. lies in the fact that it is eminently suitable for the materials used. The walls are rough stucco. Above, casement windows are set in a hand-adzed timber frame. The path and the platform before the door are of* *rough flat stones laid irregularly. To suit these elements, the simplest sort of entrance was devised. The door is set in a deep, shadowy recess. Each side the walls are rounded and the span above has a slight curve. Foundation planting adds to the effect.  A. J. Thomas, architect*

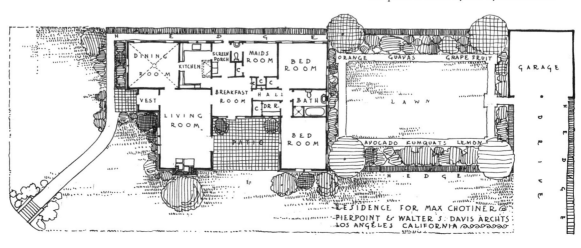

The home of Max Chotiner, Los Angeles, Cal., is a style that would harmonize with any locality. Tan stucco and many-tinted shingles give it color. Pierpoint & Walter S. Davis, architects

The two gable wings which are seen from the street flank a tiled patio. The mass of the house from this direction, as well as from the entrance front, presents an easy and very pleasing profile

This bungalow-cottage is built on a good one-floor plan. The wings are placed so that the breakfast room gets the first rays of the morning sun, and the patio is shaded from afternoon heat

A

CALIFORNIA

HOUSE

IN STUCCO

The home of Fred Smith, at Baldwin, L. I., is a pleasant adaptation of Colonial styles to the modern small house problem. The front sweep of the roof is a feature that gives the house unusual character

The kitchen wing and porch include interesting details—a brick chimney stack advanced beyond the face of the wall with a decoration lattice and a brick floored porch enclosed with lattice between the pillars

# IN THE COLONIAL STYLE

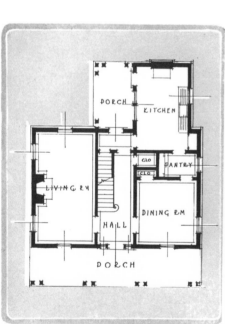

Downstairs the rooms are arranged in the simplest possible fashion. There is a house-depth living room on one side the hall, with dining room, pantry and kitchen on the other

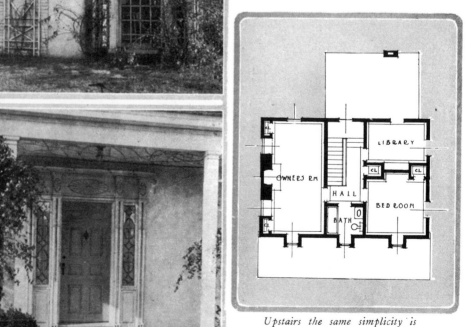

Upstairs the same simplicity is found in the disposition of rooms. Two bedrooms and a bath are provided with a small library in the rear. Such a house is adequate for the beginning family

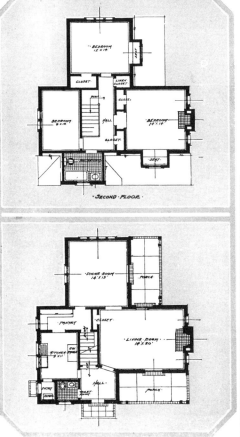

*The adaptability of English cottage styles to the American suburban house is proven in the home of G. W. Warhurst, at Philipse Manor, N. Y. It is of cream-colored stucco on hollow tile with red brick sills and borders around the doors.*

# A SIMPLE

# SUBURBAN HOME

*As the house occupies a corner plot, it is designed to have a porch on both streets. The chambers, the living and dining rooms each has three exposures, affording good circulation*

*The garage is built into the house, a modern necessity that does not destroy the illusion of the architecture. It is close to the kitchen end*

*Rough troweled stucco covers the walls, giving them a pleasant variety of light and shade. The roof is of shingles laid to simulate thatch in effect and left in their natural silver color. The bedrooms are in this end with the casement dormer windows*

*The house is L-shaped, one and a half stories in one end. The end shown here contains the living room. It has a rough wall with rounded eaves*

## LITTLE ORCHARD FARM

### WHITE PLAINS, N. Y.

FRANK J. FORSTER, *Architect*

*The feature of the plan is the combined living and dining room with its rough plaster walls, exposed beams, cottage furniture and gay chintz*

*There is nothing imposing about the entrance door—just a little corner shadowed by a flat awning and marked out by a pavement approach*

*A path of flagstones let into the grass leads up to the entrance, the grass growing between the stones. Around the foundation is a planting of colorful perennials. The house sits low, shadowed by trees*

# AN ENGLISH COTTAGE
## ADAPTED FOR AMERICA

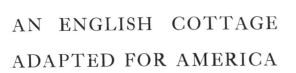

*Viewed from the highway the house presents a finely balanced façade; super-
imposed clusters of three windows each in the center and well sized, interesting doorways at each end, all set in a surface of roughly textured, warm
toned stucco under a strip of coral colored tile roof*

*At one side of the tile paved patio a
fireplace, sporting a brilliant overmantel medallion, has been built*

*From the hills beyond the house a
stream flows down a cascade into an
arched, tile bordered grotto, thence
into a pool below*

*The entrance doorway has a finely decorated flaring reveal, while the door itself is a heavily battened bit of typical Spanish design*

## A HOUSE IN HOLLYWOOD

### STILES O. CLEMENTS

*Architect*

*The driveway curves up to the house from the highway between an evergreen hedge on one side and banks of Roses and other flowering shrubs on the other*

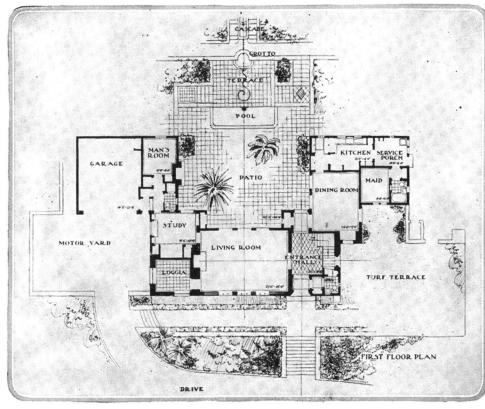

*The first floor plan shows the main part of the house devoted to the entrance, living room and study, and a wing apiece, flanking the patio, form the service and garage*

MODERN

ADAPTATIONS

*of the*

ADOBE

*A terraced adobe house at Santa Fé, N. M., built after the manner of Pueblo Indian homes. The "vigas" or ceiling beams are exposed. The windows are an American adaptation*

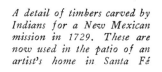

*A Spanish home of six rooms, with wings flanking a center living room. The garage joins the house on the left. The house is at Albuquerque, N. M.*

*The arched openings on the front porch, the tile covered gate and the walled courtyard distinguish this Spanish house at Albuquerque, N. M.*

*A detail of timbers carved by Indians for a New Mexican mission in 1729. These are now used in the patio of an artist's home in Santa Fé*

*The pueblo house, built in adobe or sun-baked clay, is native to New Mexico. Its revival as a style for homes in that section is noticeable*

**EL PORVENIR
THE HOME
OF MISS
EMILY KEENE
DENVER
COLORADO
M. H. *and* B. HOYT
*Architects***

*In this little garden house there is more to declare it at once Spanish than architects usually attain in modernizing and adapting the type. The Spanish house achieves its best expression through the architect's restraint*

*A closer view, showing the picturesque possibilities of the kitchen door, reveals no conspicuous details, but does reveal the architects' excellent appreciation of the colloquial traits of the style of the Spanish Missions of California*

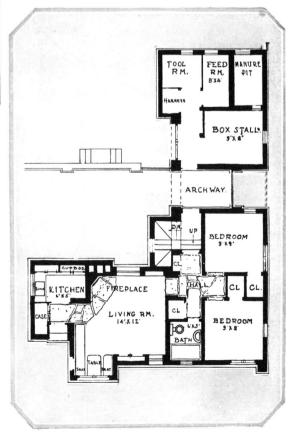

*The archway between house and stable affords a striking illustration of the rich possibilities in design that may be obtained with plain masses, plain walls, and arches*

*The plan possesses an attractive quality of informality which practically comprises the impossibly primitive adobe dwelling of early days and the modern bungalow*

Sigurd Fischer

## THE ENTRANCE FRONT

*A whitewashed brick wall broken by an easy flight of steps to a grass terrace; simple brick piers surmounted by decorative lead peacocks; rhododendrons in corners:— of such elements is made this entrance to the home of Bertrand Taylor, Jr., Locust Valley, L. I. The house is stucco painted white. H. T. Lindeberg was the architect*

Gillies

*The English cottage was architectural ancestor to the home of H. Harris, Mt. Vernon, N. Y., as is shown in the half-timber, the dip of the roof and the pleasant ranges of casement windows. Lewis Bowman, architect*

*Though the house is small, the rooms are commodiously arranged both upstairs and down*

*The entrance is tucked away in the angle formed by the living room and the enclosed porch*

Gillies

*The garden side sparkles with a fine va-
riety of materials: weather stained marble
masonry in the lower walls and piers, tile
arches in the loggia, half-timber and stucco
in the main gable, and brick-filled half-
timber in the living room wing at the right*

*The garage gable is weatherboarded in
wide elm planks which tone to a silver-
gray and whose edges are not finished
off but left in their natural irregular
shape with only the bark removed. A
bird house sits jauntily at the peak*

*The entrance is set within the interior angle
of the building and its treatment is more
severely Tudor than the rest of the house.
The stone here is local marble that has
been exposed to weather in an old foundation for near a century with splendid effect*

# A HOUSE IN
# STONE *and* TIMBER

### AT BRONXVILLE, N. Y.

The timbers in the walls of the hallway are not a mild deception and a merely pleasant decoration, but are actually working members in the structural scheme of the house, a fact which gives them a more than superficial beauty

# AN EXAMPLE OF AUTHENTIC DESIGN

LEWIS BOWMAN, *Architect*

Like the timbers in the hallway, these beams in the living room, though they are made more consciously decorative by discreet carving, are not fake, not tacked to the ceiling, but form most of the framework which supports the roof

The plan of the house was made roughly y-shaped in order that it might fit snugly the topography of the site. Such a general plan has resulted in an unusually interesting room arrangement and a departure from complete rectangularity

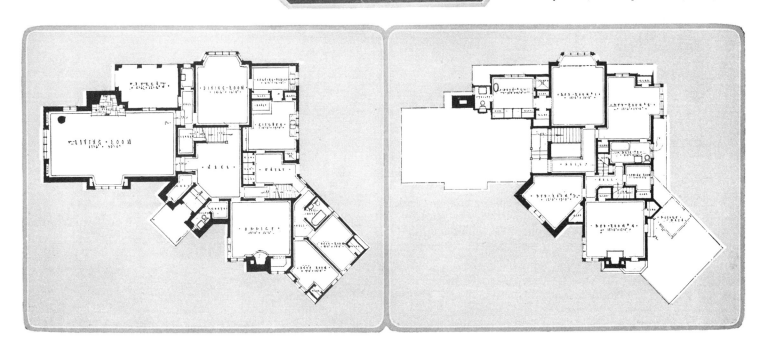

*In this house at Scardale, N. Y., the architect, being the owner as well, has indulged his
fondness for early building methods and craftsman-made materials. Most of the oak timbers
were cut in the neighborhood in 1812*

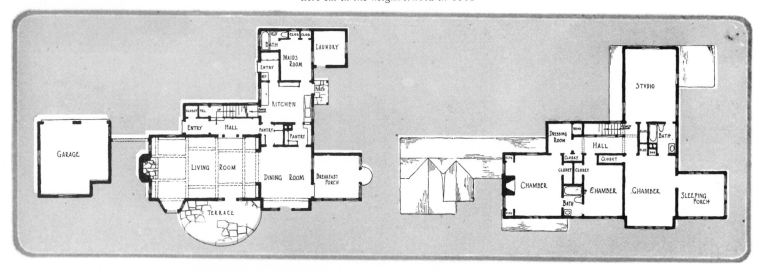

*Wherever old materials could
be used, and were obtainable,
they were incorporated in
the house; old leaded glass,
old hardware from Southern
France, old wrought iron
from Spain*

*The roof is laid up of hand-
split and hand-stained shingles. Against it and against
the old oak, the lead of
the gutters and leaders is
particularly effective in color
and texture*

*A glance at the beam indica-
tions in the living room on
the plan gives a hint of the
consistency between interior
and exterior. In the dining
room a small stage has been
**provided***

# A
# HANDMADE
# HOUSE

WALTER PLEUTHNER
*Architect*

# TWO HOUSES
# FOR SEASHORE
# OR SUBURBS

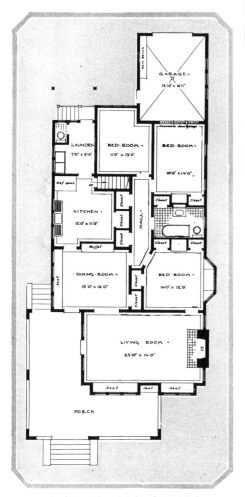

*For the site that is flat the bungalow is a logical choice. It especially lends itself to summer living. An example is found in the summer home of Amos Birdsall, Jr., at Toms River, N. J. The walls are white stucco over frame. The wood trim is stained a reddish brown and the roof a light brown*

*An interesting detail of the Bird-sall bungalow is the connection of house and garage. The plan responds to the demands of a deep, narrow lot. Heacock & Hokanson, Architects*

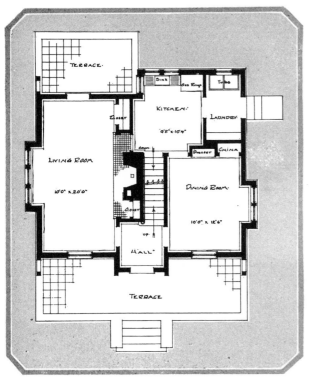

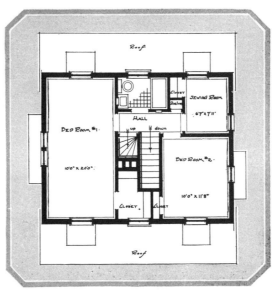

*An unusual variation of Dutch Colonial, suitable for the suburbs, is found in the home of Donald Folsom, at Sharon Hill, Pa. White walls and trim with blinds painted bottle green give it a cheerful aspect. Folsom & Stanton, architects*

*By recessing the fireplace and projecting the bay window directly opposite, the living room has been given greater width. On the upper floor not an inch of space has been wasted. The owner's room is commodious, with light on three sides*

Kenneth Clark

# A  GRACEFUL  COLONIAL  INTERPRETATION

*The Colonial style in southwestern Connecticut
has always held close to the classic idea. Here it
follows precedent but gains lightness and grace
through the use of slender columns and delicate
details. The house is near New Canaan, Connecticut; and Clark & Arms were the architects*

*The residence of Dr. E. F. Cady, at
Southern Pines, N. C., is mainly a
one-storied structure, with shingled
walls and roofs and details that are
evidently of Colonial origin*

# A BUNGALOW

# FOR THE SOUTH

## AYMAR EMBURY, II,

*Architect*

*The garage is con-
nected with the kit-
chen wing by an arch-
ed passage and its
roof repeats the kit-
chen gable, making
the group a pleasing
architectural unit*

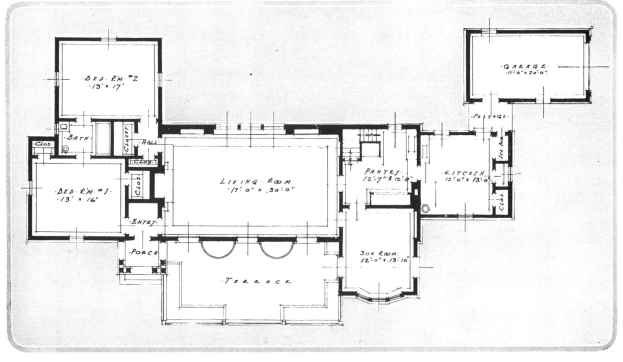

*A large living room
occupies the middle
of the house with
chambers on one side
and service on the
other. The plan is
desirable for its sim-
plicity and its livable
qualities*

The plain walls of the living room contrast
nicely with the chintz of the curtains and slip
covers. The furniture has been chosen and arranged for restful, informal beauty

The house, below, is one of twin houses facing
each other across the circle of a drive. It is a
Colonial adaptation done in wide faced shingles
stained a silvery gray

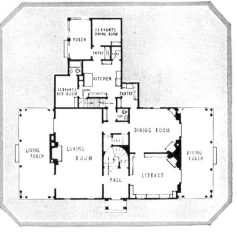

The first floor plan shows the service
section kept completely to the wing in
the rear, a spacious porch at either end,
and an interesting hallway with a
semi-circular flight

## THE HOME OF

## F.  TRUBEE  DAVISON

*Locust Valley, L. I.*

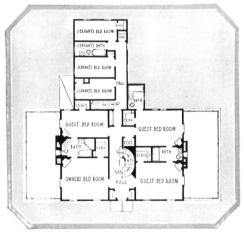

One of the delightful features of the
second floor is the fact that each principal bedroom contains a fireplace.
There are three bathrooms for the
four bedrooms

The opposite end of the living room holds the
fireplace with its comfortable furniture group
and a stunning hooked rug. Above the mantel
hangs a Colonial convex mirror

The owner's study, with its desk, its shelves of
law books, and its wall of photographs achieves
a personality quite as interesting as that of any
conscious decoration

# DESIGNED BY

# WALKER & GILLETTE

*Architects*

Tebbs

*There is great beauty in the architectural treatment of the living room—in the fine fluting of the mantle, pilasters and cornice, and in the proportions of the traditionally uncurtained Georgian windows*

*At the left is shown part of the dining room in the Draper house. The corner cupboard is set beside the entrance from the hall and provides most of the ornamental architectural detail in the room*

*The choice and grouping of furniture and the handling of the decoration have been done with splendid feeling for the refinement and simplicity of the living room's interior architecture*

The doorway and the loggia with
its Ionic columns and lovely balustrade above form an unusually
successful bit of architecture in the
spirit of the Georgian designers

The house is a nice mingling of formality and informality. The latter
quality is felt in the broken outlines
of the plan and the disposition of the
sharply sloping roofs, while the
former feeling pervades practically
all the details. The front façade is
entirely, but very gracefully, formal

Although the principal rooms of the
house are found on one floor, their arrangement is such that no confusion
could possibly exist. The bedrooms
become a perfectly isolated group
with the principal entrance from the
main hall, through the stair hall, with
a service entrance from the kitchen

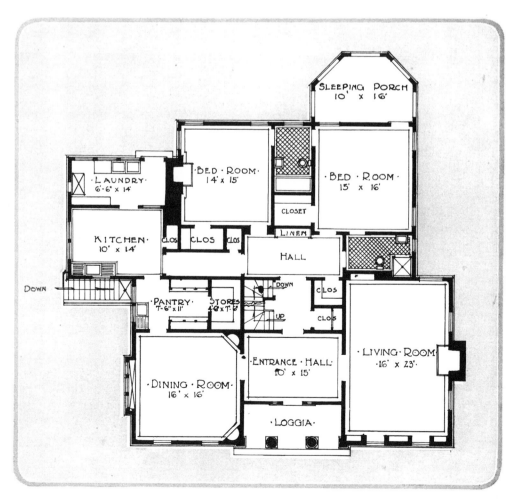

# THE HOUSE OF MRS.
## JESSE DRAPER

### ATLANTA, GEORGIA

HENTZ, REID & ADLER
*Architects*

*The garden front of the house faces a broad turf terrace that lies at the floor level and is held in place by the stone retaining wall. Two small gardens flank this terrace, running out from each of the gable wings, and steps descend from them to the garden on the level in the foreground*

*The arched openings onto the semi-circular lower garden space are so arranged that from either side they frame a vista that ends upon the gable wing opposite. The design of the arch itself is noteworthy for its slender and graceful simplicity and its appropriateness in the architectural scheme*

# A

# COUNTRY HOUSE AND

# GARDEN

AT NEW CANAAN, CONN.

*Essentially the same in mass as the garden side, the entrance front is altogether different in feeling. Where one by its broad terrace and French windows encourages a sense of ease and makes an intimate connection with the gardens, the other suggests just the right degree of dignity*

*The garden side of each gable wing opens upon a little garden whose central panel is a long rectangular pool. The second floor of the wing contains a sleeping porch whose windows, under the pediment, extend almost entirely across its width. A lattice is an important feature of the façade*

# IN

# MODERN CONNECTICUT

## COLONIAL

**CLARK & ARMS,** *Architects*

Gillies

# A LIGHT AND LOFTY PORCH

*This two-story porch with its tall slender columns is typical of western Connecticut, and shows how architecture adapts itself to customs and climate. Here the heavy, dignified classic portico idea has been made lofty and shallow to provide more light and air. H. T. Webster, the cartoonist, owner, Wesley S. Bessell, architect*

Duryea

*This house was so designed and placed as to command a panorama view of the Hudson River. Its one story has been found advantageous in that all rooms are well ventilated and the attic affords storage space*

## THE HOME OF EARL BEYER, SCARBORO, N.Y.

PATTERSON-KING, *Architects*

*Shingle walls painted white, roof of dark tobacco brown, blinds and entrance door painted Wedgwood blue, and window boxes filled with flowers make this a colorful little house. The chimneys are of white stucco*

*Cross ventilation and light are found in all rooms. The garden is enclosed by a wing of the house and a pergola of corresponding length. The garage is part of the house itself. The house is equipped with all modern conveniences*

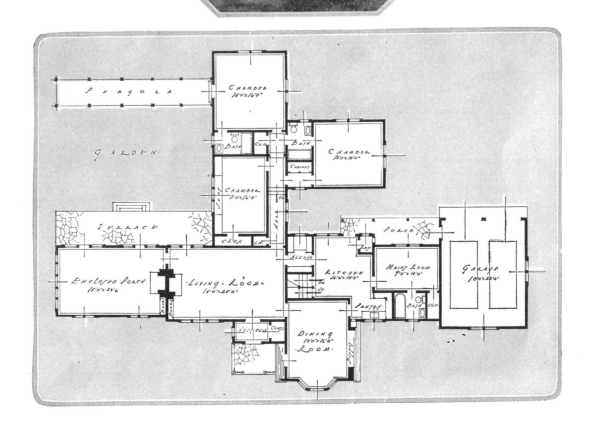

*This French door with its finely designed fan-piece offers a splendid contrast between the weathered texture of the shingled façade and its delicate sophistication*

*The feeling of intimacy with its site is aided on the garden side of the house by the two projecting bays which also work into a nicely balanced window grouping*

*The view of the house above on the opposite page shows the garden side and the long, glass enclosed sun porch which opens off the living room*

*Covered with hand rived shingles, the house presents the texture as well as the architectural style of the old Dutch houses in the neighborhood*

# THE HOME OF MRS. JEANNETTE R. GILLIES

## FLUSHING, N. Y.

### TREANOR & FATIO, *Architects*

*The main doorway, with its fluted pilasters and broken pediment, has all the charm and dignity that lie in the Colonial handling of the Doric order*

*Though the house is one of moderate size there is roominess on both floors. The arrangement on the service side is particularly splendid*

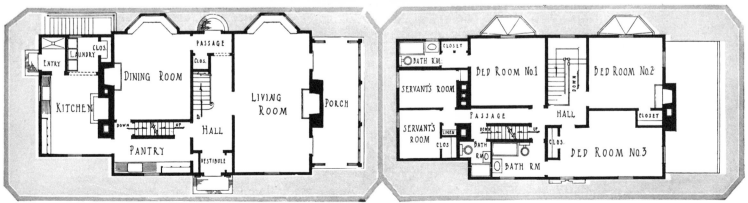

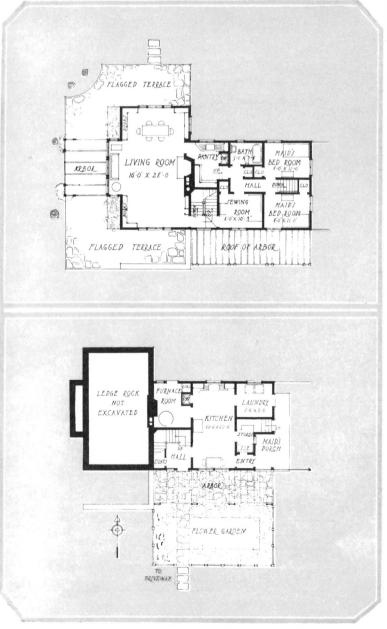

Clark

*The home of Miss Spokeman, at Washington, Ct., owes its effect to inherent good proportion and placement. The matched boarding exterior is painted in a deep tone of pink, with green shutters—an unusual color scheme*

*The plans show a special study of the grades on which the house is built. Bedrooms are upstairs, and all the service accommodation is on the living room level, and below that floor. Murphy & Dana were the architects*

# A SHIPLAP HOUSE

### in

# CONNECTICUT

The residence of Hugh McCulloch, at Springfield, O., is a modified Dutch Colonial design with interesting end porches that give the house a pleasing low line and additional size. It is in white painted shingles with green blinds, a satisfactory combination for a Colonial house

There is abundant space in this five-room house. Entrance is effected through a front door opening directly on the living room. Upstairs the two bedrooms are ample and the stairs are kept small. The inside trim finish is cream enamel. Hall & Lethly were the architects

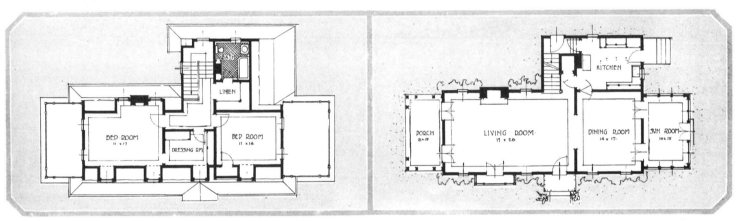

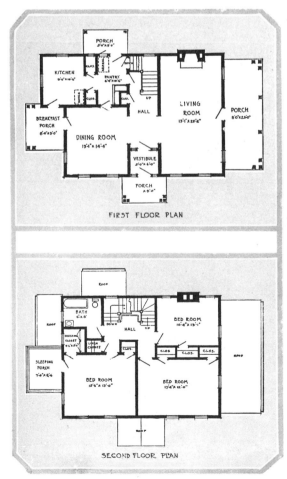

FIRST FLOOR PLAN

SECOND FLOOR PLAN

Another type of Colonial design is found in this seven-room house. A house-depth living room occupies one side, with hall, dining room and service completing the ground floor, C. H. Gilbert, architect

The walls are of broad Colonial siding painted white; the roof, which is of shingle, is left to weather. There is a porch on each side, giving a balance to the house and additional living space

# TWO SHINGLED HOUSES

*The idea for these delightful small houses at Larchmont, N. Y., sprang from some Colonial cottages on Cape Cod. Simplicity of design gives them distinction*

*In this particular cottage colony the materials vary from clapboard, shingle and shiplap to stone. Like the exteriors, the interiors are done in the Colonial manner*

*Simple and inexpensive as they may be these houses exhibit no sign of commonplaceness. They are filled with architectural freshness and original ideas in efficient planning*

This one is done in clapboard, with quite a Colonial air; the doorway being a particularly fine piece of unpretentious design. Casement windows are used throughout all the whole group

Each house contains five rooms: a living room, two bedrooms, bath, combination porch and dining room, and small kitchen. All have full cellars underneath and some attached garages

# CAPE COD IN WESTCHESTER COUNTY

C. C. MERRITT, *Architect*

## SHINGLE FOR COLO-NIAL HOUSES

*The home of Reginald E. Marsh at Bronxville, N. Y., is a Colonial design in stained hand-split shingles, green shutters and a roof of rough green slate. Porches at each end give the house balance. The front suite of bedrooms is arranged for the master and children*

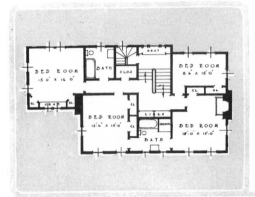

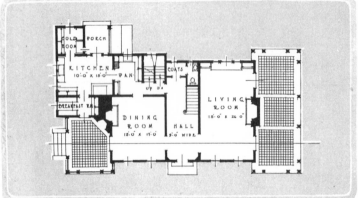

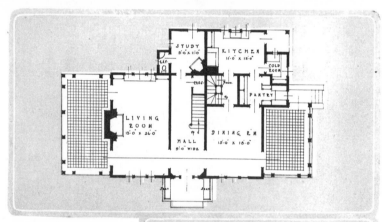

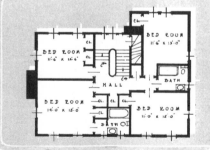

*The plans of these two houses are similar, except that they are reversed. They are built side by side with the living porches facing each other. Although the color schemes are the same, from the exteriors one would not realize that they are similar in plan. Tooker & Marsh, architects*

*The house of Thomas B. Gilchrist at Bronxville, N. Y., has a stucco first story and hand-split shingles above. The roof is of green slate, and the shingles are stained. A Germantown hood separates the stucco from the shingles. This style is especially suitable for a setting among the trees*

# A BALANCED PLAN FOR

# COMFORTABLE LIVING

*A generous second floor plan, this, five bedrooms, three baths and two maid's rooms with an abundance of closet room and a large stairs hall*

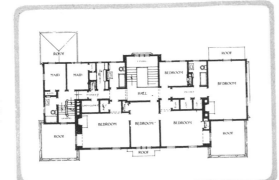

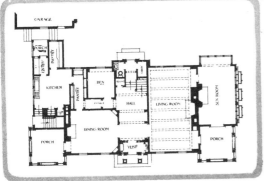

*Two porches balance the design, one off the dining room and one off the living room. A sunroom adds to the size of the living room*

*The exterior of the house is a balanced Colonial type that can be executed in either shingles or clapboard painted white*

*Lattice, on which vines will grow, decorates the wall of the garage. Decorative urns are placed on top at intervals*

*A long narrow hall upstairs gives access to the four major bedrooms and to the bath at both ends. Maids' rooms are over the kitchen*

*This type of house is economical in that the shingles are left to weather, or could be stained, and only the trim painted. The entrance in the corner is a feature that is both saving of space and unusual*

# A HOUSE WITH AN

# L-SHAPED PLAN

*The first floor plan has two distinct parts —the service and dining room and the large living room, terrace and porch, with a flower room at the back*

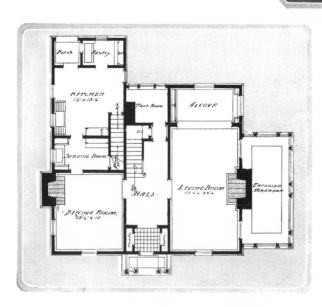

The overhanging second story with decorative pendant finials is a type to be found in very early New England houses. It accords harmoniously with this modern interpretation, a house found at Hartford, Conn., a type suitable for the suburbs or restricted country districts

At the rear of the living room is an alcove, giving added space, and at the end of the hall a plant room, both unusual features for a small house. The kitchen and pantry are both of generous proportions. Note the plant room

Without the decorative latticed entrance portico the front façade would be unpleasantly austere. Its projection from the house creates desirable shadows and its arched top is a relief to the otherwise straight lines of the house. Smith & Bassette, architects

# EARLY

# NEW ENGLAND

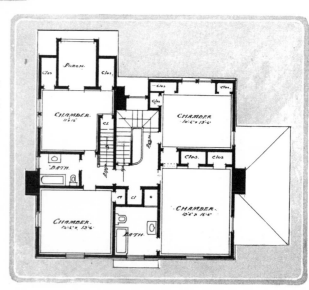

Four bedrooms and two baths are provided on the second floor. The plan is balanced. A servants' stairs leads up conveniently from the serving room

## A SMALL HOUSE IN VIRGINIA

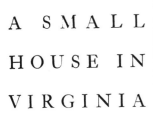

*The deep, low eaves of the front are repeated at the side of the house where a hood, handled in a similar fashion, covers the dining room bay and the kitchen entrance porch*

*The home of George L. Street, Jr., in Richmond, Va., sits snugly behind its white paling fence with the charming air that accompanies long roof lines and deep set eaves*

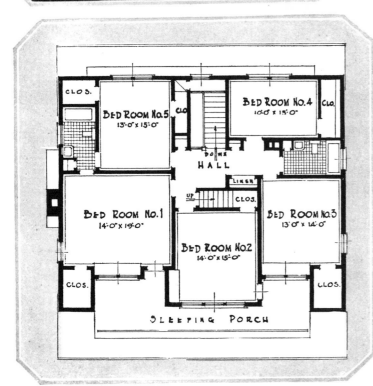

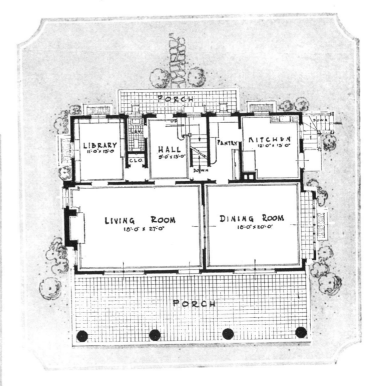

*The five bedrooms on the second floor are entered from an interior hall, thereby effecting a fine economy of space. There are two baths, and a closet to a room*

*The living and dining rooms take up the entire garden side of the house, which is separated from the lawn by a wide, tiled porch. W. Duncan Lee was the architect*

Tebbs & Knell

*Few small houses achieve such distinguished formality as this without dwindling out of scale. Here the result is delightfully successful. The Ionic portico, usually associated with buildings of grander proportions, has been brought nicely into the architectural scheme, as well as the surmounting balustrade*

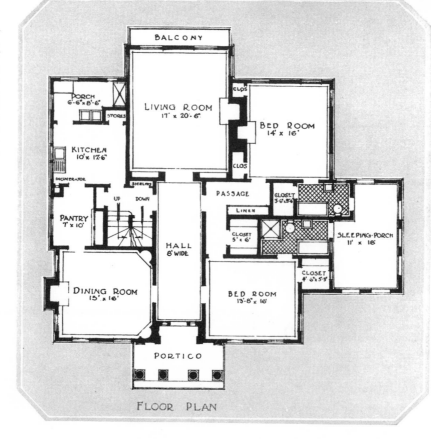

FLOOR PLAN

# A
# SMALL HOUSE
# OF FINE
# FORMALITY

*Hentz, Reid & Adler*

*Architects*

*Practically the whole house has been fitted onto one floor. A central hallway, connecting the portico with the living room in the rear, separates the dining room and service section from the sleeping quarters on the right. Hunter Perry, Atlanta, Ga., owner*

Tebbs & Knell

*The small hall has been given distinction by an interesting wall paper and a nicely balanced group of furniture consisting of an 18th Century chest of drawers and painted cottage chairs*

*The living room with its finely proportioned paneling and commodious built-in bookshelves is made colorful by an Oriental rug and gay chintz covers on the comfortable overstuffed chairs*

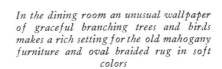

*In the dining room an unusual wallpaper of graceful branching trees and birds makes a rich setting for the old mahogany furniture and oval braided rug in soft colors*

*One wall in the dining room has been finished in smooth plaster painted a neutral tone. This makes a nice contrast to the wall paper and a dignified background for the classic lines of the overmantel*

# F L O W I N G   R O O F S

*The roof is the fluid element of house design. It can sweep down, as this sweeps, from a high peak, to cover the lower level of the wing and shadow the open porch. Contrasting with these are the more reposeful parts of the design. H. T. Lindeberg, architect*

# PLANS FOR HOUSES IN THE SPANISH AND DUTCH COLONIAL MANNER

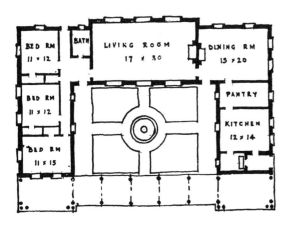

*The Spanish type, suitable for the South, Southwest, and southern California, is built around three sides of a patio, with the fourth side enclosed by a pergola. Stucco walls and red tile roof would be used. All the rooms, of course, are on the one and only floor*

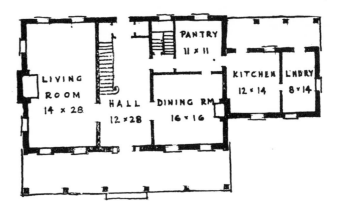

*Dutch Colonial is a deservedly popular type. It has long, low picturesque lines, rests comfortably on the ground and can be erected in a number of materials—shingle, whitewashed brick, clapboard, stone and hollow tile*

*The Dutch Colonial type of house generally calls for a central hall running through the middle of the house, with a house-depth living room on one side and dining room and service on the other. The plan provides a servants' stairs*

Tebbs & Knell

*From the garden side the house seems to nestle comfortably in a deep and luxuriant setting. Vine-clad and mellow with age its dignified form shows no trace of austerity*

*A garden has been made on a level space below the house level at the rear. Box-lined paths connect it with the building and broad stone steps make an easy descent*

*The richly colored marble mantel in the living room, its mirror, clock and ornaments, are, like the furniture, typical of the Empire taste which came with the Greek Revival*

# THE GREEK
# REVIVAL
# IN GEORGIA

Tebbs & Knell

The air of dignity and calm in this great portico, with its fine Doric shafts and simple cornice is an argument for a revival of the Greek Revival. Neel Reid, owner

The garden, only recently completed, has two panels in knots and parterres and a central section, brick-paved, marked by a long narrow pool between beds of Irises

The entrance hallway repeats the scheme of decoration found elsewhere in the house: a panel of Lafitte paper framed above an Empire chest holding two alabaster figurines

## HOME OF NEEL REID, ARCHITECT

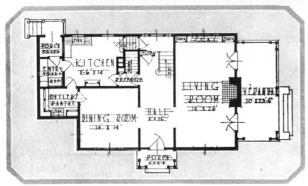

*Stucco over expanded metal or hollow tiles makes a permanent house with a pleasing wall surface. A slight extension set back from the front line of the house gives commodious service quarters on the first floor. William T. Marchant was the architect*

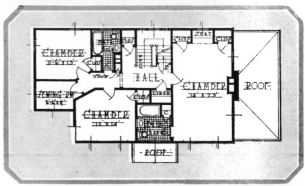

*This house was designed to create a distinctive small house for a reasonable sum. It is executed in shingles painted white, a shingle roof, green painted shutters and red brick chimneys. Lattice gives the front porch the relief of design. Aymar Embury, II, architect*

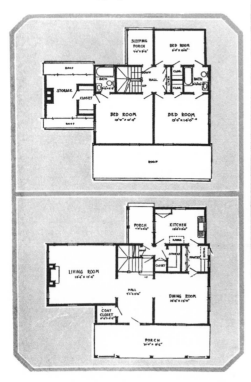

# FOR SUBURBAN
# OR COUNTRY DISTRICTS

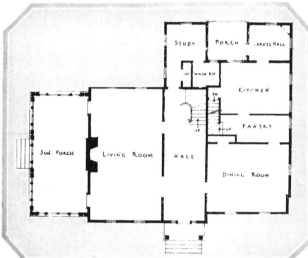

*From the naïveté of its original state this farmhouse has been very successfully given an architectural consciousness, with a hooded entrance, balustraded wings and shutters in the old New England manner*

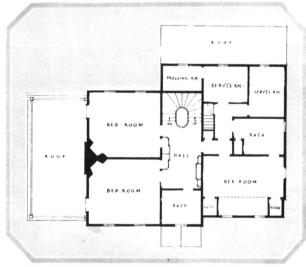

*The first floor has a living room of splendid proportions, with windows at either end and French doorways leading onto a sun porch. The right wing contains the dining room, study and the service*

*The stable, gardener's cottage and smaller buildings have been done over delightfully; the former into a garage with three arched doorways, and the latter into a group having the fine flavor of unpretentious design*

*On the second floor are two master's bedrooms, one guest's, two for servants, two bathrooms and a pressing room. The hallway is wide and is connected with the one below by a curving staircase*

# A REMODELED FARMHOUSE

### ERIC KEBBON, *Architect*

Gillies

Nothing emphasizes quite so well the close attachment of the house for its site as the ease with which one may step from lawn to floor level. Here, to the porch, it is a matter of five inches, and one feels, from the window heights, that the living room, in its low wing, is settled just as snugly

## THE DUTCH COLONIAL

*home of*

MRS. G. F. McQUADE, FREEPORT, N. Y.

The living room is a space of splendid proportions on the plan, roof high, and lighted from three sides; the hall is generously sized and forms a fine connection between all the rooms and entrances of the first floor

A detailed view of the living room wing shows the materials of the house and their treatment. The walls are shingled and stained white; the bricks of the chimneys are painted white and the solid paneled shutters are apple green. The evergreen planting of tall Conifers may soon be too robust

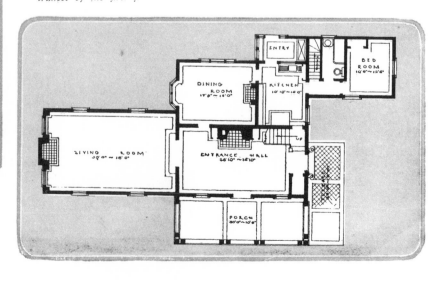

Gillies

*The view from the entrance angle proves that the main doorway to a house may be casually placed, architecturally speaking, yet be extremely effective. In the immediate foreground is a large Maple that has just been moved to this new location lending it shade, age and luxuriance*

# IN MODERN DRESS

*designed by*

DWIGHT JAMES BAUM, ARCHITECT

*With the two wings running through but one story, the second floor seems that of a smaller house. The baths are well disposed, the bedrooms are of good, comfortable size, and the closet space is unusually ample*

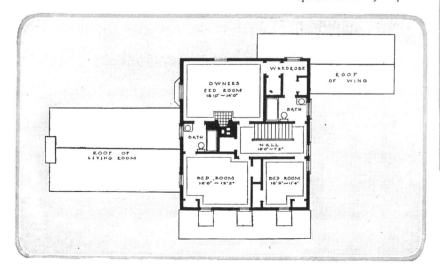

*The entrance doorway, with its fine elliptical fan light, its well proportioned panels, and its slender pilasters, contains the same gracefulness which characterizes so much of Mr. Baum's work. Without some diverting it is possible that the Wistaria may soon smother much of this delicate architecture*

Nicholas

# STRENGTH AND INGENUITY

*Log cabins are enjoying a vogue. In forest camps and on country estates they seem equally at home. And the building of them, when the builder has an appreciation of rough timber, offers unique opportunities for the exercise of strength and ingenuity, virtues found in this door. The cabin is on the estate of Byron B. Horton, Barnes, Pa., and was designed by Carl Gildersleeve*

Albert A. Nicholas

*This cabin in the Pennsylvania mountains is a splendid example
of what fine beauty of form and texture can be obtained with
well selected logs and skilful workmanship*

# LOG CABINS AS HOLIDAY HOUSES

*A Primitive Form of Backwoods Architecture which
Provides An Ideal Retreat from Too Much Civilization*

THE log cabin is in many ways the ideal holiday house. It represents a return to the primitive, a complete escape from everyday living. No number of conveniences can destroy its essential ruggedness or its frontier flavor. When it rises in the clearing from which its timbers have been taken it stands as an almost irresistible lure from sophistication. It is architecture gone back to nature, and it provides a way for people to go there too—in comfort.

A cabin can be built in a woodlot not far from the house, or at any distance from home in whatever sort of wilderness. The situation requires for its effectiveness but one thing, and that is an adequate supply of lumber in its natural state. The wild charm of a log cabin depends upon a setting which will make a *log* house seem the only sensible solution of a building problem.

The appropriate place, then, for a log cabin is in the woods. No other site

will do. But aside from having the little building actually belong to its situation there are certain other necessities which should be provided. These are: water, sunlight, and a view. Without a spring or stream close at hand cabin life takes on great difficulties. A well would obviate the necessity of running water, as would, of course, a piped supply. But these, particularly the latter, smack strongly of acute civilization, and might in time suggest still other and more modern conveniences that in the end might change completely the original cabin character of the place.

The matter of sunlight is apt to be slighted in the woods, but it is even more essential there than elsewhere.

*The cabin doors are made of rough
pine slabs, weathered, with hinges
and cleats of hawthorn. The axe-
hewn cleats are fastened to the doors
with pegs made of hornbeam*

*Here is what might be called a rugged interior, but the craftmanship is so marked and the treatment so sensitive that the effect is one of great beauty*

*The porch posts, rails and rafters are of unpeeled Birch. Byron Barnes Horton, owner, Barnes, Pennsylvania; Carl Gildersleeve, designer and builder*

Aside from the cheerfulness it brings it keeps the cabin dry and prevents the decay which would come with constant dampness in the roof and timber walls. In the same way there is a practical side to a view, for a cabin densely surrounded would not only lack wider horizons for the eye, but, without openings to catch the prevailing breezes, might find itself stifled on warm, windless days.

The cabins shown here are a splendid example of what can be done in this primitive architecture. They have all the backwoods flavor together with the refinement of line and detail which comes with a sense of beauty and careful workmanship. Both on the exterior and interior can be seen how fine an effect is possible when the logs in the walls are all straight and well matched for size. Here is a regularity that can never be monotonous, for two logs can never be perfectly alike. Each one has a somewhat different character—

Nicholas

a different color and shape.

The logs are unpeeled; and it would be difficult to find more beautiful color and texture than in rough logs. They are locknotched at the corners where they come together with a slight but effective unevenness in their length. The spaces between the logs are chinked with cement in such a way that the effect is of a cleanly raked, deep joint. The comparatively even line of the logs separated by this narrow, inset line of almost white cement is extraordinarily decorative, both inside and out.

Practically all the timber used in these cabins is in its natural state or has been hewn out with an axe. The exception to these two primitive building methods is contained in the floors, roof, windows and door frames. The floors are of pine, matched and weather stained. The roof sheathing is of weather stained spruce boards covered with red cedar shingles, or asbestos roofing paper, both excellent for the purpose.

*Well back from the lake, the smoke shows even here the wind's force. Consequently the clearing should be large enough to prevent sparks starting forest fires*

*There should not be a too strict regularity in the length of the logs. This unevenness adds to the picturesqueness of the cabin. Darragh Aldrich architect of cabins shown on this page*

*Above is an example of the stockade method of cabin building, with vertical logs set on the heavy sill timbers*

*An important thing about cabins is the view. Be sure to have a large enough porch set toward that best exposure*

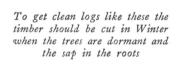

*To get clean logs like these the timber should be cut in Winter when the trees are dormant and the sap in the roots*

*The wide overhang of the roof makes a splendid shelter for the porch and protects the doorway from driving rain*

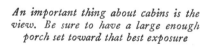

The garage and chauffeur's quarters are cleverly disposed in this brick and half-timber building on a New England estate. It is really built on the wall. Below is a view of the other side

Simple and yet architecturally pleasing is the garage on the place of G. C. Price, at Charleston, West Va., of which Dennison & Hirons were the architects

The Tudor aspect of this garage and chauffeur's quarters is taken from the architecture of the house, the home of F. R. Ford, Essex Falls, N. Y. Michael Stillman was the architect

The outside stairs are pleasantly featured on the garden side of the garage which is shown above. Small pane windows are in harmony with the brick and half-timber

*The contour of the land and the location of the house decided the position of this three-car garage on the level below the middle section. It is on the place of Paul C. Krochle, Euclid, Ohio, of which Dercum and Beer were architects and William Pitkins, Jr., landscape architect*

# LARGE AND SMALL
# GARAGES
# IN VARIOUS
# SIZES

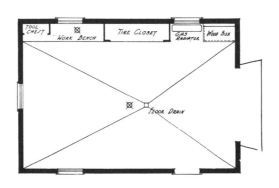

*An ideal arrangement for a one-car garage, with bench closets, etc. ranging down one side. Inside measurements of sixteen feet by twenty-four will accommodate one car and this working equipment*

*Barns that are remodeled for garage purposes, such as this example, require architectural ingenuity to give them character. A. C. Holden & Associates, architects*

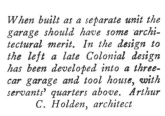

*When possible the garage should be attached to the house and should share its architectural style. Above the earliest American type of architecture has been applied to even so modern an appendage as a garage. A. J. Thomas, architect*

*When built as a separate unit the garage should have some architectural merit. In the design to the left a late Colonial design has been developed into a three-car garage and tool house, with servants' quarters above. Arthur C. Holden, architect*

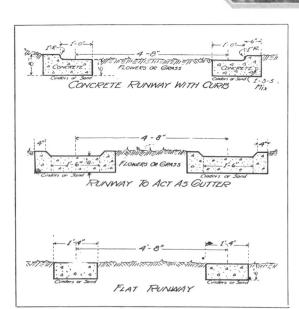

*Three types of garage run ways are shown to the left, together with necessary measurements and construction*

*Each kind of driveway has its own practical feature. It should be 9 to 10 feet wide with a 15 foot flare at the entrance*

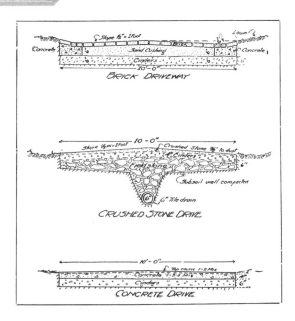

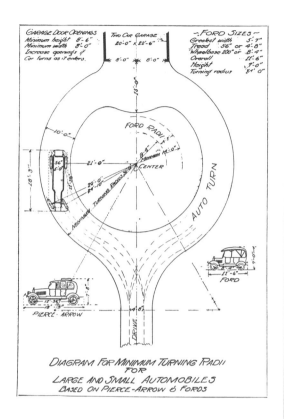

The size of the turnaround depends on the wheel base of one's car, using the Ford as a minimum. At the top of the chart are measurements for garage door openings and for a two-car garage

# GARAGES AND

# DRIVEWAYS

Even the Spanish type of house native to California does not defeat the architect's ingenuity when it faces the attached garage. In the home of Craig Heberton, Montecito, Cal., the garage shares the character of the house. George Washington Smith, architect

Each type of lot presents a different problem in locating the garage. Do not make the approach to it too conspicuous. Use a circular turnaround where space permits; otherwise plan for a Y-turn which necessitates backing the car

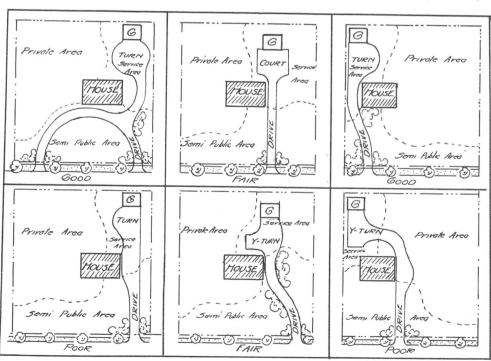

# THE HOME BUILDER'S QUESTIONNAIRE

*Answer the Following Questions, and You Will Have a*
*Comprehensive Idea of the House You Plan to Build*

HOUSE & GARDEN'S Information Service receives many questions from prospective builders which are difficult to answer because of the form in which they come to us. Very often the really helpful answer to a question depends upon the answers to other questions, or upon data and information not given by our correspondents. The following questionnaire is intended as an outline of the things to be considered by anyone who proposes to build a house, and their sequence is important as a guide to systematic thinking. In another issue we will publish a questionnaire on the alteration or remodeling of old houses.

1. What is the maximum amount of money available for the building of the house? *If the available amount for expenditure is limited, give due thought to the possibilities of "progressive building", that is, of planning your house so that its essential living accommodations can be built immediately, and other portions of it at some future time.*

2. What is the nature of the site? Level? Hillside? Country? Surburban? Village? Mountain? Seashore? *The answer to this question would largely dictate the answer to Question 3.*

3. What is your preference, if any, as to architectural style? Colonial? Italian? Spanish? English? What kind of English —manor house or cottage? Bungalow?

*The answer to this question would have a good deal to do with the answer to Question 4. Questions 2, 3 and 4 are all closely related. The site considered topographically, and the site considered sociologically, as a location, with certain neighborhood obligations, should govern the choice of style. Style, in turn, usually governs the type of construction of a house, and the type of construction calls for certain materials.*

*If there is no special style suggested by site or neighborhood, the possession of a certain kind of furniture might dictate the style. No one would put a collection of fine Colonial and Early American mahogany in an Italian villa.*

4. What type of construction have you in mind? Frame? Brick? Stucco on frame? Clapboards on frame? Half-timber? Varied construction, utilizing varied materials? What kind of roof? What material? *A consideration of type of construction is inseparable from the consideration of materials to be used, and the exterior finish, such as paint, stain, etc.*

5. How many rooms on the first floor? *The answer to this will govern the answer to Question 6. The first-floor plan usually determines the extent of the cellar, and also the floor area available for the second story.*

6. What is to be accommodated in the cellar? Laundry? Garage (if grade permits)? Preserve Cellar? Workshop? Is the site one in which surface water drainage into cellar must be specially provided against? *If so, waterproofing must be used on the foundation, an extra cost not usually included in estimates.*

7. What type of heating plant is your choice? Hot Water? Steam? Hot air? Pipeless? Fuel oil? *Prospective builders should not be too much influenced in the choice of mechanical equipment of any kind by unprofessional advice. Failure of equipment to perform properly is often due to poor installation by local mechanics, and has no bearing on the real merit of the machine.*

8. What do you plan for arrangement of first floor? Hall? Hall and Living Room combined? Reception Room? Music Room? Library? Dining Room, or Dining Alcove off the Living Room? *(This is more suitable for the cottage or bungalow than for the larger house, and if you already have furniture, the plans should be studied accordingly.)* Porches? Sun Parlor? Terraces? Breakfast Porch?

9. How about details of first floor? Flooring? Wall finishes? Fireplaces? Type of windows? Doors? Lighting fixtures? Hardware? *If no local dealers carry designs in stock which appeal, designs may be selected from the catalogues of various manufacturers, and ordered through local dealers or through the contractor.*

10. How about the Kitchen? Large or small? Movable or built-in equipment? Kind of range? *Answer to Question 6 tells whether or not laundry tubs are to be in Kitchen.*

11. Will there be a separate Pantry? A Refrigerator Room? A Maid's Room near the Kitchen on the first floor?

12. How many rooms upstairs? Sleeping Porch?

13. Any rooms other than Bedrooms? Nursery? Sewing Room? Store Room?

14. How many family Bedrooms? How many **Guest Rooms?**

15. How many Bathrooms? What grade of fixtures will be wanted for these?

16. Any rooms on third floor? If so, what are they?

17. Linen closet? Other special closets?

18. What wall finishes on second floor? Plaster finishes or wall paper? What kind of flooring? Doors? Windows?

19. What lighting fixtures on second floor? Hardware?

20. What type of garage? *(See Question 6.)* If a separate building, how many cars? A mere shelter, or a finished building, with chauffeur's quarters, heating plant, etc.?

21. Are there any special features to be considered in your house? Large pieces of furniture? Window seats? Built-in furniture? *If you already have certain large pieces, such as a davenport, a large bookcase or anything which would not fit the average wall space, it is well to make notes of its dimensions, so that these can be figured on the plan.*

22. Are you contemplating features not included in building estimates based on standard construction and equipment? Copper rain-leaders and gutters? Brass plumbing pipe? Casement windows? Window screens? Weather strips? Special mantels? Paneling?

*It is well to keep in mind from the start that the decision to have special equipment will mean added cost, but that it will also enhance the value and satisfaction of your house. It is also important to remember that special materials or equipment, decided on after the cost estimate for the whole house is made, cannot be expected to be covered by that original estimate.*

23. Is the question of electric outlets best studied after the house plans are definitely decided on?

*When every point enumerated above has been duly considered, the memory can be relieved of considerable burden, and the danger of forgetting important details can be eliminated by making a set of lists. These may be made either by rooms or by subject. Thus, a set of lists by rooms could be made to cover every item contemplated for the Living Room, every item for the Dining Room, and so forth. A set of lists by subjects could be made to cover, for instance, all the hardware, itemized by rooms and all the plumbing and lighting fixtures, itemized by rooms. These lists, as the work began to take definite form, would probably be subject to revision, but they would afford a definite means of recording in a systematic way all changes in decision, all substitutions, eliminations or additions.*

# ADDRESSES OF CONTRIBUTING ARCHITECTS

Albro, Lewis—deceased

Aldrich, Darragh....701 Kenwood Parkway, Minneapolis, Minn.

Barber, Donn.................101 Park Ave., New York City

Baum, Dwight James, Waldo Ave., Riverdale-on-Hudson, N. Y.

Behr, F. G...............100 E. 45th St., New York City

Bessell, Wesley.................58 W. 49th St., New York City

Bodker, A. J.,.................37 W. 57th St., New York City

Bottomley, W. Laurence...........112 E. 55th St., New York City

Butler & Corse.................10 E. 44th St., New York City

Clark & Arms.................137 E. 46th St., New York City

Clements, Stiles O., 1124 I. N. Van Nuys Bldg., Los Angeles, Cal.

Cross & Cross.................385 Madison Ave., New York City

Dana, Richard H., Jr............350 Madison Ave., New York City

Davis, P. & Walter S............3215 W. 6th St., Los Angeles, Cal.

Dennison & Hirons............288 Lexington Ave., New York City

Dercum & Beer.................4500 Euclid Ave., Cleveland, O.

Dominick, Wm.................19 W. 44th St., New York City

Embury, Aymar, II............150 E. 61st St., New York City

Emory, W. H., Jr............615 Munsey Bldg., Baltimore, Md.

Folsom & Stanton.................10 S. 18th St., Philadelphia, Pa.

Forster, Frank J............33 W. 42nd St., New York City

Gilbert, C. P. H.............1 Madison Ave., New York City

Gildersleeve, Carl, % Morse & Morse....247 Park Ave., N. Y. C.

Hall & Lethly.................806 Fairbanks Bldg., Springfield, O.

Heacock & Hokanson...........1218 Chestnut St., Philadelphia, Pa.

Hentz, Reid & Adler...........92½ N. Forsyth St., Atlanta, Ga.

Holden, A. C.................101 Park Ave., New York City

Hoyt, M. H. & B.....200 Colorado Nat'l Bk. Bldg., Denver, Colo.

Johnson, Reginald D..........100 E. Colorado St., Pasadena, Cal.

Kebbon, Eric.................522 Fifth Ave., New York City

Lang, Eugene J.................19 W. 44th St., New York City

Lee, W. Duncan.................Traveler's Bldg., Richmond, Va.

Leland, Joseph D.................41 Mt. Vernon St., Boston, Mass.

Lewis, Schell.................101 Park Ave., New York City

Lindeberg, Harrie T.................2 W. 47th St., New York City

Marchant, W. T.................36 Pearl St., Hartford, Conn.

McMurray, Donald D., 480 California Terrace, Pasadena, Cal.

McGoodwin, Robert.................34 S. 16th St., Philadelphia, Pa.

Merritt, C. C.................138 E. 44th St., New York City

Okie, R. Brognard.................1420 Chestnut St., Philadelphia, Pa.

Palmer, E. L.................513 N. Charles St., Baltimore, Md.

Patterson-King.................435 Lexington Ave., New York City

Peabody, Wilson & Brown..........140 E. 39th St., New York City

Pitkin, William.................4500 Euclid Ave., Cleveland, O.

Pleuthner, Walter.................132 E. 40th St., New York City

Redfern, Harry, State Management Districts,
Central Office, Whitehall, S. W. 1, England

Sanger, Prentice.................21 E. 40th St., New York City

Smith, George Washington........17 Mesa Rd., Santa Barbara, Cal.

Smith, O. B.................501 Fifth Ave., New York City

Smith & Bassette........Connecticut Mutual Bldg., Hartford, Conn.

Smith & May.................Calvert Bldg., Baltimore, Md.

Soule, Murphy & Hastings......1206 State St., Santa Barbara, Cal.

Stillman, Michael.................34 W. 50th St., New York City

Thomas, A. J.................15 E. 47th St., New York City

Tooker & Marsh.................101 Park Ave., New York City

Treanor & Fatio.................3 E. 44th St., New York City

Walker & Gillette.................128 E. 37th St., New York City

Warhurst, S. W.................Philipse Manor, N. Y.